LIFE
LEADER

LIFE LEADER

Finding the Greatness Within

Dr. Jonathan Mayhorn

WESTBOW°
PRESS
A DIVISION OF THOMAS NELSON
& ZONDERVAN

Scripture quotations are from The Holy Bible, English Standard Version® (ESV®), copyright © 2001 by Crossway, a publishing ministry of Good News Publishers. Used by permission. All rights reserved.

WestBow Press books may be ordered through booksellers or by contacting:

WestBow Press
A Division of Thomas Nelson & Zondervan
1663 Liberty Drive
Bloomington, IN 47403
www.westbowpress.com
1 (866) 928-1240

Because of the dynamic nature of the Internet, any web addresses or links contained in this book may have changed since publication and may no longer be valid. The views expressed in this work are solely those of the author and do not necessarily reflect the views of the publisher, and the publisher hereby disclaims any responsibility for them.

Any people depicted in stock imagery provided by Thinkstock are models, and such images are being used for illustrative purposes only.
Certain stock imagery © Thinkstock.

ISBN: 978-1-4908-5211-9 (sc)
ISBN: 978-1-4908-5212-6 (hc)
ISBN: 978-1-4908-5213-3 (e)

Library of Congress Control Number: 2014916757

Printed in the United States of America.

WestBow Press rev. date: 9/26/2014

Contents

Acknowledgements

I have a motivational poster with a picture of the Lincoln Memorial sitting in my office with these words written on it, "The essence of leadership is vision." When I read those words every morning it makes me realize that no vision can be implemented by a leader without the help of those who believe in that vision. Just like Abraham Lincoln had to rely on a select few who bought into the vision of keeping the country together, the same holds true for implementing the vision of what a life leader is. The five basic aspects of becoming a life leader wouldn't have made it past my back porch if it weren't for the original group of life leaders; Drew, Scott, Ben, Ryan, and Guy who helped me unleash a hidden passion.

Great ideas are only effective if you put them to use. I wouldn't have written a book on becoming a life leader if my wife hadn't encouraged me to just go for it. Thank you to Kelli for supporting my ideas and for watching our three young children so that I could write over the course of eight months.

When trying to translate the ideas in my mind to words on paper I often would reach out for help. There is one person who went above and beyond the call of duty to read and edit the paper every week. Without him, a life leader would not have been properly defined. A special thanks to Mitch for using our weekly social gatherings to read and edit all of those drafts.

Also, thank you to my brother Josh for the help with the physical fitness workouts as well as advice on that chapter. Your ideas are amazing and you truly have a gift. I still use these workouts every week and the results are very beneficial.

Finally, a thanks to the two professors from Regent University who edited the original manuscript back in 2008 and 2009 so that I could meet the requirements to become a Doctor of Strategic Leadership after four long years. I am ever grateful to Myra and Cornè for their feedback during this process.

Chapter 1

The Need for Life Leaders

It was a moment I will never forget. During the summer of 2005, my friends and I were having one of our many conversations on leadership. We talked about life, relationships, school, jobs, and the future. Throughout the dialogue, one idea was resounding above all others. As we sat on my back porch, everyone told stories about the poor leaders-be it professors, bosses, or even their own parents they had come across in their lives and how they did not want to follow in their foot steps. Then right there, just as countless times before, my brain and heart launched the vision of how a new type of leader could make a difference in the world. I began describing in detail what this leader would look like and how he or she could go about changing the lives of others. This person would impact the world around him or her by living out the principles that followers look for in every aspect of life. After this, we settled on a name to match the type of person I was describing; it was quite simply "life leader." This title has stuck with me and developed into a passion to write a book geared toward inspiring an entire generation of leaders to make a real difference by not using the same ineffective behaviors they have been exposed to from other poor leaders.

Like my friends on that porch, everyone reading this can name someone who gives leadership a bad name. This person could be a CEO, pastor, politician, or principal. These individuals whom society has classified as leaders are not perfect and, as a result, often do things that let their followers down. Each time leaders get caught in a scandal or the pursuit of their own greed, it is their followers who suffer most.

Since the world has numerous leaders who are failing to live up to ethical standards and others who are simply passive and unprepared to lead, we are faced with a leadership deficit that needs to be filled. This deficit does not only apply to those with authority but can also include every man or woman who has the chance to influence those around him or her on a daily basis.

The reason for such a large leadership deficit can also be attributed to how people are taught to lead by their organizations. By studying leadership theory, I have learned which theories work best and which ones are not as effective. The baby boomer generation (born between 1944 and 1961), happen to make up the majority of current leaders and are accustomed to transactional leadership. It is important that aspiring leaders learn about this type of leadership to better understand others and to know why it isn't always effective. From a study on transactional leadership, I have found that it will not provide the success in retaining younger followers. Even so, many leaders are still using it today and helping to contribute to the leadership deficit.

Leaders who practice transactional leadership guide followers in the direction of established goals by clarifying roles and task requirements. They motivate followers by appealing to their own self-interest. Transactional leadership principles motivate by the exchange process, in that leaders expect the accomplishment of tasks as well as good relationships from their followers in exchange for giving them rewards they desire.[1] For example, corporations usually exchange status and wages for the work effort of an employee. Aspiring leaders may find that many organizations still use transactional leadership behavior to one degree or another. However, it is important to remember that a leader should never exclusively or primarily use transactional leadership behavior to influence others. A few problems with utilizing only transactional leadership include: using it as a tool to manipulate others for selfish personal gain; placing too much emphasis on the bottom line; being short-term oriented with the goal of simply maximizing efficiency and profits; and pressuring others to engage in unethical or amoral practices by offering strong rewards or punishments. Transactional leadership may seek to influence others by exchanging work for wages,

---

[1]   J.M. Burns. *Leadership,* (New York: Harper & Row, 1978).

but it does not build on the follower's need for meaningful work, tap into his or her creativity, or meet any of the other very diverse needs that today's younger workers may have. When used as the primary behavior by a leader, it can lead to an environment permeated by position, power, perks, and politics. Everything is based on results and not on the development of future leaders to take over for the aging baby boomers.

A more effective and beneficial leadership behavior to achieve long-term success and improved performance with the Mosaic generation (born between 1979 and 1996) and Generation X (born between 1962 and 1978) might be *transformational* leadership. Transformational leadership is about implementing new ideas to solve critical problems. Leaders who practice transformational leadership continually change themselves, stay flexible and adaptable, and continually improve those around them. The two theorists most often associated with transformational leadership in its modern state are James Burns and Bernard Bass. In his book, *Improving Organizational Effectiveness through Transformational Leadership*, Bass talked about the fundamental theoretical qualities that define transformational leadership from its polar opposite, transactional leadership.[2] Before him, James McGregor Burns wrote his Pulitzer Prize-winning book entitled *Leadership*.[3] In his book, he described qualities transformational leaders possess in different fields of endeavors ranging from the military to business to politics.

According to Bass, leaders who are transformational in nature possess the qualities of charisma, vision, intellectual stimulation, and inspiration. Transformational leaders, who are charismatic and visionary, appeal to followers' ideals and moral values and inspire them to think about critical problems in new or different ways. Transformational leaders also inspire followers to transcend their own self-interest for the good of everyone in the group. Research indicates that transformational leadership, as compared to transactional leadership is strongly correlated with lower turnover rates, higher productivity, and higher follower satisfaction.

---

[2]   Bernard Bass. *Improving Organizational Effectiveness through Transformational Leadership*. (Newbury Park, CA: Sage Publications, 1994).

[3]   J. M. Burns, 1978

With transformational leadership, each follower is coached, advised, and delegated some authority. As Burns put it, transactional leadership does not foster a relationship that "binds leader and followers together in a mutual and continuing search for a higher purpose."[4] Transformational leadership on the other hand revolves around the concept of the leader shifting the values, beliefs and needs of the followers and both raising each other's motivation and sense of higher purpose. The higher purpose is achieved when the ethical aims and aspirations of leaders and followers merge into one.[5] To fill the leadership deficit with a new generation of leaders, I would like to combine the qualities of a transformational leader with those of a servant leader. There was one great teacher in history who taught how to do this in an ethical way, and that was Jesus Christ.

As a servant leader, Jesus showed two clear points of leadership: a visionary role and an implementer role.[6] As a visionary, Jesus did the right things with a focus on results, and as an implementer, he did things right. The three things that are needed in vision are purpose, preferred picture of the future, and values. Jesus stated his vision when he told his disciples to be "fishers of men," and not "fishermen."[7] Jesus had a clear picture of the future, as he knew that he ultimately would die for people's sins. He also had core values as he cited and ranked these values starting with two commandments, the first and foremost being, "Love the Lord your God with all your heart and with all your soul and with all your mind,"[8] and the second being, "You shall love your neighbor as yourself."[9] This second value is often difficult to commit to, because many leaders do not love their followers. One way to overcome this is to act your way into feeling love for another. As the philosopher Immanuel Kant would say, we can try to achieve moral worth by acting

---

4   Ibid, 1978.

5   Bryman, A. *Charisma and leadership in organizations.*(Newbury Park, CA: Sage Publications, 1992).

6   Ken Blanchard and Phil Hodges. *The Servant Leader.* (Nashville, TN: Thomas Nelson, 2003).

7   Matt. 4.19 English Standard Version (ESV).

8   Matt. 22.37 (ESV).

9   Matt. 22.39 (ESV).

out the value of love.[10] The best way to model servant leadership as part of becoming a better leader is to copy the ultimate leader, Jesus Christ.

While it is true that some people have dreams to reach grandiose leadership positions in order to be known as a great leader and leave a legacy, those lofty dreams do not always come true, as people find these authoritative positions are held by a select few transactional leaders. So what are individuals left to do when they realize they may never reach these levels of leadership? Do they decide that being a leader wasn't meant for them and accept that their fate is in the hands of others? The answer to these questions and many others can be answered as one learns how to find the greatness within and use it to become a leader in all types of roles and stages of his or her life.

By reading this book, one will find that leadership is not just reserved for a select few transactional leaders at the top of a business, church, political party, or school. Rather, it is something that is obtainable by everyone who works hard for it. Webster's dictionary defines the word *leader* as "one that leads."[11] In looking up the word *lead,* one will find that it simply means "to guide or conduct; hence to direct in action, thought, or opinion."[12] According to this definition, whenever you are guiding others or directing their actions, thoughts, and opinions, you are really leading them. Those who are guided are considered followers at that particular moment. In order to guide followers consistently over time, an individual must learn to develop the skills necessary to become a special type of leader called a life leader. This leadership style that will be taught combines the best transformational and servant principles to benefit followers.

A life leader is someone who leads in every aspect of their own life so effectively that others they come into contact with are motivated to action and inspired to follow. The key to becoming a life leader is to work on every aspect of one's own life first. As an individual develops these aspects they will soon discover that others will be motivated to not only follow but also to become a leader of their own lives. This is an important point because most people are caught up in living their

---

[10]   William H. Shaw. *Moral Issues in Business.* (Australia: Wadsworth, 2001).

[11]   *Webster's New Collegiate Dictionary* (1956), s.v. "leader."

[12]   Ibid.

own life not knowing that others are watching their actions, words, and deeds and deciding whether they want to follow such a person. If others are watching and even following, wouldn't everyone want to be the best guide they could be? This relationship between follower and life leader is not to be taken lightly. Life leaders, contrary to mainstream leadership principles, do not allow their role to be used for personal gain, but rather for the benefit of a higher calling that allows them to better serve others. The motivation behind this is that balancing each facet of one's own life first leaves a person with a maturity level that allows them to have more to offer others. Life leaders are not those who excel in their careers but neglect their health or family to reach success. Nor are they superhuman in that all parts of their life are perfect. Rather they are normal people who work hard in their life using a balanced approach that benefits their family, co-workers, and followers.

The journey required to become a life leader is not an easy one though. If people are looking for a quick fix to become a successful leader, then they will be disappointed with life and this book. Many have read leadership materials that give instructions to follow to become a better leader in the workplace. This, however, is not the sole focus of this book. Instead, the purpose is to teach everyone how to learn to become a leader within the context of everyday life and then encourage others to do the same consistently. This will require a change in attitude, behavior, perspective, and even daily routines. The difficulty in making these changes is that the demands of today's society have left most people with a hectic life that is based on unfulfilling routines. There are careers to navigate, families to keep up with, schools and churches to attend, and social activities to squeeze in during the little time that is left. So the correct question should not be, "Will this book make me a better leader within my career?" Rather the correct question is, "Can this book and the ideas proposed propel me into becoming a healthier person in all areas of my life?"

Like most development initiatives, becoming a life leader is not going to happen overnight as it takes continual improvement in the many areas of one's life. The methods required to become a life leader are often overlooked since they require a lot of hard work. Why have they been overlooked by emerging leaders? The analogy that comes to mind to explain this is found in the poem, "The Road Not Taken" by Robert Frost.[13] In this poem the author writes about two paths that diverge in the woods. The person in the poem must choose a path to take without knowing what lies at the other side. They chose to take the road less traveled and that was what made all the difference. Today when most people come to a crossroads in their life they take the easiest path and stay away from the path less traveled for fear of straying from their routine or comfort zone. This leads to becoming stuck in the same job, habits, and lifestyle but always expecting different results. To become a life leader an individual *must take the road less traveled*, which does not mean a person should pursue a chaotic path in their life. Instead they should follow a road that is filled with good habits and methods such as the ones that will be taught and referred to as the holistic approach.

The Holistic Approach

The word holistic in our society has often been given a bad wrap, especially in the world of medicine. In actuality the word itself is not bad at all. It is defined by Webster's as, "emphasizing the importance of the whole and the interdependence of its parts."[14] In terms of a person the important parts that are dependent upon each other to make up the whole are the following: the spiritual, emotional, mental, physical, and social aspects. A person who is working towards becoming a better leader must continually develop all of these aspects together throughout their life in order to effectively use the holistic approach.

Being strong in one or two areas and weak in the others does not allow anyone to become well balanced. Nor does it allow people to reach their full potential or prepare to lead others they come into contact with. We all know of a spokesperson, be it a pastor, politician, or instructor, who is intellectually gifted but unable to relay information effectively as they are gifted, due to lack of social skills in delivery. Similarly a leader within the workplace may be knowledgeable, emotionally strong, and physically fit but have very little spiritual traits that allow them to

---

[13]   Robert Frost, *Mountain Interval* (New York: Henry Holt and Company, 1920), 75.

[14]   Webster's, "holistic."

show patience, compassion, and self-control to their followers. Are the employees that work for this leader more likely to follow and respect that person's decisions if they can't even show patience, compassion, and self-control? At the same time an individual does not have to master all five aspects to become a life leader. Rather it is a balance of them all followed by a commitment towards continual improvement that allows for the best chance of positively influencing their own life and guiding others to do the same.

The holistic approach to becoming a life leader focuses on the importance of the whole person; however, it breaks this up into five interdependent parts that need to be explored further. Each part will be explained in terms of why it is important and how to become more fit in that particular area. There will also be assessments placed at the end of each chapter to help the reader determine how fit they currently are. Finally, there will be space provided to allow everyone to write down specific steps they will take as well as goals they have to improve their assessment score. Below is a brief overview of the five interdependent parts:

1) *Spiritual fitness* which encompasses developing your spiritual side throughout your life. This includes embracing the fact that you were created to be a spiritual being by establishing a close relationship with God.
2) *Emotional fitness* which involves developing a firm foundation, balancing and prioritizing your life, and investing in others emotional development.
3) *Mental fitness* which includes developing the mind to prepare for the challenges one will face. This area will focus on one's thinking style, the importance of gaining good knowledge, and how to use the entire brain to make the best decisions.
4) *Physical fitness* which includes eating healthy and exercising to develop the body needed for life's challenges. Being physically fit provides a good foundation for many of the other aspects.
5) *Social fitness* which focuses on developing a life outside of work, church, or school. One will learn the importance of

embracing two different groups of people in order to grow as a person and leader.

After all of the above aspects are discussed, you will learn how to utilize the holistic approach to become totally fit. It is important that you continue on this journey and fill out the assessments as they provide a way to develop custom built growth plans for becoming a life leader. The consequences for not taking the time to read the chapters and fill out the assessments are that you will continue to live your life just as you are now. This means that there will be no written plan for growing in the five areas of life: spiritually, emotionally, mentally, physically, and socially. Behaviors and habits will not have been changed, and your road map for leading others will be based on how your own leaders treated you. No one wants to be a poor leader, but many people do not know how to be a good leader. All they know is what their mentors or parents have shown them. It is time to break free from the vicious cycle of developing more poor leaders in the world. Come and join a new group of people who choose to be great leaders in all aspects of life. Then, when you are well on your way, you can start to develop other life leaders. My challenge to you is to read and apply the principles found in the chapters that follow. I believe your life will never be the same!

Chapter 2

Spiritually Fit

To learn how to develop all aspects of one's life using the holistic approach, you must know the importance of each interdependent part. The first aspect which is often overlooked is actually one of the most important parts to becoming a life leader. This involves developing your spiritual fitness. Life leaders have a back bone in spirituality, because they know God created them for a certain purpose in life. As you progress through this chapter you will see that spiritual health is simply unleashing the greatness that God has given you in order to benefit and encourage others. By establishing a better relationship with your Creator, you can tap into the gifts God has given you to serve others. Often though people ask, "What does it really mean to be spiritual and what does that have to do with leading my own life or the lives of others?" To answer this question we must first define what we mean by spiritual.

Webster's dictionary defines the word spiritual as, "of or consisting of spirit."[15] To be spiritual is to be someone that expresses their spirit. People often confuse this definition with expressing themselves through human designed rituals such as meditation, art, or dance. In actuality it should involve expressing the spirit in ways God originally intended. To learn to develop your spirit you must first understand why you were created to be a spiritual being in the first place. To explore this further we can look at the sixth day of creation in the first book of the Bible. On this day God had just finished creating all of the living creatures that

---

[15]   Webster's, "spiritual."

dwell on the earth and then turned His attention to humans. Let us pick up the story in Genesis 1:26, "Then God said, let us make man in our image, after our likeness. And let them have dominion over the fish of the sea and over the birds of the heavens and over the livestock and over all the earth and over every creeping thing that creeps on the earth."[16]

The next verse in the book of Genesis continues to talk about the image we were created in as it states, "So God created man in His own image, in the image of God He created him; male and female He created them."[17] Both verses clearly state that God created people in, "His own image." He patterned humans after himself. But what does "His own image" really mean since we do not know what God looks like? In the book of John, Jesus gives us the answer by stating, "God is spirit and those who worship Him must worship in spirit and truth."[18] From this we see that God's image is in the form of a spirit and requires us to worship Him in spirit. When we compare Jesus' declaration in John to the statement made by God in Genesis, we can clearly see that man, who is similar to God (created in his image, but still dependent on Him), possesses an immortal spirit. It is in this likeness to God, "being a spiritual being," that distinguishes mankind from the rest of creation.

Other great authors have touched on this subject, such as Henri Blocher who stated in his book, *In the Beginning*, "mankind was created as the living image of God, in a quasi-filial relationship with him and, like him, endowed with the spirit."[19] In the New Testament of the Bible the apostle Paul agreed as he wrote, "for a man indeed ought not to cover his head, since he is the image and glory of God."[20] Humans were created to worship God using the spirit He had given them, thus people are truly spiritual beings. The other thing that we can learn from the creation verses is that humans were created to have a ruling capacity.

---

[16] Gen. 1.26 English Standard Version (ESV).

[17] Gen. 1.27 ESV.

[18] John 4.24 ESV.

[19] Henri Blocher, *In the Beginning*, by David Preston (Downers Grove: Intervarsity Press, 1984), 90.

[20] 1 Cor. 11.7 ESV.

From the beginning, God handed over the leadership of the world to human kind, thus the phrase "to have dominion over."[21] God designed us to have a ruling capacity on earth because we are reflected in His image. The problem is however, as humans that are capable of sinning we tend to go our own way instead of following God's original design for our life. By sinning we are turning our back on the ruling capacity that we were given. How do you embrace that ruling capacity as a life leader? By accepting the fact that you were created to be a spiritual being that is dependent on God.

Since we were created in "His own image" we are considered to have the capability to develop our own spirit as we draw closer to Him. God as the ultimate spiritual being is known to display what are called the fruits of the spirit. It is up to us to develop a relationship with Him in order to become spiritually fit and display these nine characteristics that result from this relationship. This is easier said then done as most people can't develop these traits without a clear action plan. These nine characteristics: self control, patience, kindness, goodness, joy, peace, faithfulness, gentleness, and love were named the Fruits of the Spirit by the apostle Paul.[22] In Galatians he wrote, "If we live by the spirit, let us also walk by the spirit."[23] What he meant by this is that all humans are spiritual beings but not all people develop their spirituality enough to exhibit the Fruits of the Spirit.

One who is spiritually fit or expresses a high level of spirit is someone that displays those traits. Most people have come across at least one person in their life who exhibits all nine of the characteristics listed above. With all the difficulties that life throws at people, you may wonder where a person gets their joy, love, or any of the other characteristics. Some will say they obtain these things from going to church or by following a certain religion. If this were true then there would be large numbers of people displaying these behaviors every time they left their church on Sunday. The truth is to develop and exhibit the nine characteristics associated with being spiritually fit, you must be responsible for continually developing your own spirit. Therefore a life

---

[21]   Gen. 1.26 ESV.
[22]   Gal. 5.22-23 (ESV).
[23]   Gal. 5.25 (ESV).

leader is someone who knows how to continually develop their spiritual fitness level in order to express the Fruits of the Spirit for the benefit of others who choose to follow them. To do this effectively you need a clear action plan for becoming spiritually fit as described on the pages that follow.

Becoming Spiritually Fit

The first step to improve your spiritual fitness is one you may have already taken which is to choose to have a personal relationship with God. For those that may not know the only way to do this is to accept Jesus as your Lord and savior. Jesus himself told Nicodemus, "for God so loved the world that he gave his only Son, that whoever believes in him should not perish but have eternal life."[24] He continued by saying, "for God did not send his Son into the world to condemn the world, but in order that the world might be saved through him."[25] Jesus was letting everyone know that He is God's only son and that people must believe in him to be saved from their sins and to have eternal life in heaven. Jesus later reconfirmed this to his disciples when he stated, "I am the way, and the truth, and the life. No one comes to the Father except through me."[26] Being made in the image of God we are born with a God shaped hole in our lives. When we ask Jesus into our lives to wash away our sins we start to fill this hole while beginning a powerful transformation. We try to fight off our old sinful ways and fill our lives with activities that draw us closer to God. This transformation is difficult however, and can be compared to undergoing surgery without anesthesia. To have success in growing spiritually we need to know the tools that God has given us to make the transformation less painful. If you have already accepted Jesus Christ as your savior then you can move on to the second step to becoming spiritually fit which is developing and utilizing the resource of prayer.

Prayer is one of the few resources available to everyone in the world. When we go to a quiet place and pray to the Lord we are engaging in a

---

[24]   John 3.16 ESV.

[25]   John 3.17 ESV.

[26]   John 4:6 ESV.

conversation with Him. To effectively communicate with God we must realize that there are two very important parts to that conversation. The first is when we talk; God is listening and can hear our concerns. Prayer can be used as a vehicle to voice things that we do not have control over or as an admission of our own inadequacies. Often people forget the second part of a conversation is one that actually requires listening. When we are silent in prayer we can let God speak to us. To develop a relationship with our Creator, prayer should be used daily. If you do not know how to pray there are various guidelines available.

While there is no right or wrong way to pray, one set of guidelines is known as the acrostic A.C.T.S. Each letter stands for a major element from the Lord's Prayer that Jesus used teach others how to pray.[27] The letters in A.C.T.S. stand for the following:

Adoration- Spend the opening part of the prayer worshiping and adoring the Lord.

Confession- Ask for forgiveness for the sins you have committed.

Thanksgiving- Giving thanks to the Lord for everything He has done for us.

Supplication- Pray for other's needs and then your own.

There is a lot of room to vary your prayers from day to day and still communicate with God. The important thing is to make sure the prayer is heartfelt and not a ritual. Instead you should come to God as a humbled spiritual being that wants to communicate with your Creator. The third way to develop your spiritual fitness and draw closer to God is to read the Bible daily.

The Bible is considered God's written word and is one of the main ways that He speaks to us. The apostle Paul taught this to his apprentice Timothy when he wrote, "all scripture is breathed out by God and profitable for teaching, for reproof, for correction, and for training in righteousness, that the man of God may be competent, equipped for

---

[27]   Matt. 6.9-13 (ESV).

every good work."[28] Here we see that the Bible can be used as a training guide to become more righteous within our lives. The word *righteous* simply means, "Free from sin."[29] As mentioned before the only way to get rid of sin is to have a relationship with God through the acceptance of Jesus as your savior and to confess your sins. The only way to keep from sinning is to continually read His word and apply the principles learned to your daily lifestyle. By reading and applying God's word we are listening to Him and developing the relationship necessary to become more spiritually fit. Think of the Bible as your spiritual food as well as a guide to teach others how to become spiritually fed. Now that we have touched upon the main parts of becoming spiritually fit, how do we apply this to busy lives?

To answer this question let us turn to my personal story. This is the one aspect of the holistic approach that I am constantly looking for ways to improve upon. Growing up in church I knew who God was and heard the Bible being taught but I never really had a deep relationship with Him. When I got into college I stopped attending church and just focused on work and school. I did not make any time for reading my Bible or for prayer. For the most part I was considered a good person who had a decent life but something was missing. The God shaped hole was never filled and I attempted to supplement it with friendships, relationships and a constant quest for knowledge. It wasn't until nine years ago when I went through an unexpected divorce that I began to seek God to fill that hole. I was at the lowest point in my life in that it felt like I had been stripped of everything that was important to me. In actuality I had been focusing on everything but God which should have been the primary source for my spiritual health. Looking back I made a promise to God that if he turned my life around when I was at my weakest point than I would not turn my back on Him when I became stronger. Asking Jesus to come into my life again was the first step on the path to a spiritual transformation. The next step was to dig deeper into His word and learn what it means to be a Christ follower.

I began reading my Bible everyday as part of a yearly plan to go through the Old and New Testament. I soon discovered that this plan

---

[28] 2 Tim. 3.16-17 (ESV).

[29] Webster's, "righteous."

only took an investment of fifteen minutes a day to read His word and make a journal entry on how it applied to my life. This proved to be a powerful way to develop knowledge and understanding of God's plan for my life and the lives of others. In addition to this I began to make time to pray at every meal and during a quiet time in my room. The lessons I learned are that even with busy lives people can begin to connect with God by investing twenty minutes per day to pray and read their Bibles. I would like to caution that the time recommended here is just a suggestion for reading the whole Bible in a year and praying daily. This should not encourage you to take a legalistic approach to reading or praying because a set amount of time does not guarantee a better relationship with God if it becomes just another forced ritual. Just as prayer must be heartfelt, the same goes for reading His word and applying it to our lives. As life leaders become spiritually mature they find that this reading and prayer time will not only satisfy their own needs but will also allow them to pray for and share God's knowledge with others. Developing spiritual maturity is not always easy for a person new to the Christian faith. Sometimes they need a support system to guide them during their spiritual journey.

An example of this happened to me in 2005 while I was earnestly seeking a stronger relationship with God. I found a local church in Charlotte that had a 20 something's group. This group of young men and women met weekly for Bible study and monthly for social events. It was during the weekly studies that my relationship with God grew as I listened to the testimonies of others. I learned how they went through similar transformational journeys and overcame past struggles to embrace what God had to offer them. I also learned of various books, CD's, and classes that they had used to feed their quest for spiritual guidance. Spending time with other Christians can also open up the possibility for you to find a spiritual mentor.

As you work to develop your spiritual maturity you will come into contact with people who are at a higher degree of spiritual health. Sometimes a relationship will develop as you seek spiritual guidance from a seasoned believer. This process of an experienced leader relating to a less experienced individual as a teacher, counselor, and friend is known as mentoring.[30] The reason people often develop mentoring relationships is because it is a tangible means to maximize intellectual capital. This can be beneficial to an aspiring life leader as you are able to have someone to answer your questions about faith, the Bible, and God. As you develop your spiritual fitness you may even be asked to be a mentor for others at a different spiritual level. Either role is a large part of learning to guide or lead others within the spiritual aspect of your life.

Developing spiritual strength is such a critical part of being a life leader because it allows you to develop a stronger relationship with your Creator. This relationship will help you as a developing life leader to get through some tough challenges as you rely on faith in God. Being spiritually mature also helps us to guide others through their spiritual journey and even lead them using the fruits of the spirit. These traits can't be faked all the time and followers will know if a leader is authentic in expressing them. They have to come from within which in this case is a developed spirit. Now that we know what it takes to improve our spirituality, you may ask, "How do we determine what level of spiritual fitness we are currently at?" The answer is to take the spiritual assessment on the next page.

[30] Chip Bell. *Managers as Mentors- Building Partnerships for Learning*. Second Edition. (San Francisco: Barrett-Koehler publishers, Inc., 2001).

Assessing Your Spiritual Fitness Level

Rate yourself on the following questions using a scale from one to five. A one means that you currently do not focus on developing that particular aspect in your life. A five means that you are always involved with developing that aspect in your present day life.

1	2	3	4	5
Never	Rarely	Sometimes	Often	Always

Rating: 1-Never to 5-Always (Please Circle)

1. I have an active ongoing daily relationship with Jesus Christ.

   1   2   3   4   5

2. I engage in heartfelt prayers on a daily basis.

   1   2   3   4   5

3. I read my Bible for at least 15 minutes each day.

   1   2   3   4   5

4. I write what I have learned from my daily Bible readings in a journal.

   1   2   3   4   5

5. I attend a church that has relevant Biblical teachings on a weekly basis.

   1   2   3   4   5

6. I fellowship with other believers on a weekly basis in order to learn from them.

     1   2   3   4   5

7. I continue to develop a relationship with a spiritual mentor.

     1   2   3   4   5

8. I continue to develop others by being their spiritual mentor.

     1   2   3   4   5

Exhibiting the Fruits of the Spirit

A definition of each of the nine fruits of the spirit will be given. Rate yourself on the following questions using a scale from one to five. A one means that you never express that particular fruit of the spirit. A five means you always express that particular fruit of the spirit in everyday life.

1	2	3	4	5
Never	Rarely	Sometimes	Often	Always

Rating: 1-Never to 5-Always (Please Circle)

9. Self-control is defined as having control of oneself.[31] How often do you have complete control of your thoughts and actions?

     1   2   3   4   5

What type of things will you do to improve your self-control score?

---

[31] Webster's, "self-control."

10. Patience is defined as enduring trials without complaint.[32] How often do you endure trials without complaint?

    1   2   3   4   5

What type of things will you do to improve your patience score?

11. Kindness is defined as a state of being kind or showing good will.[33] How often do you show good will towards others?

    1   2   3   4   5

What type of things will you do to improve your kindness score?

12. Goodness is defined as moral excellence.[34] How often do you show moral excellence in your thoughts and actions?

    1   2   3   4   5

What type of things will you do to improve your goodness score?

13. Joy is defined as a state of happiness.[35] How often are you in a state of happiness?

    1   2   3   4   5

---

[32] Webster's, "patience."
[33] Webster's, "kindness."
[34] Webster's, "goodness."
[35] Webster's, "joy."

What are some things you will do to improve your score when it comes to expressing joy?

14. Peace is defined as having harmony in personal relationships.[36] How often do you express harmony in personal relationships?

    1   2   3   4   5

What type of things will you do to increase your score and have more peace in your life?

15. Faithfulness is defined as being full of faith in God.[37] How often do you express full faith in God and his plan for your life?

    1   2   3   4   5

What type of things will you do to improve your faithfulness score?

16. Gentleness is defined as a state of being gentle, especially in your manners or disposition.[38] How often do you express gentle manners to others?

    1   2   3   4   5

What type of things will you do to improve your gentleness score?

---

[36] Webster's, "peace."
[37] Webster's, "faithfulness."
[38] Webster's, "gentleness."

17. Love is defined as a feeling of strong personal attachment brought on by sympathetic understanding of others.[39] How often do you express a strong personal attachment through a sympathetic understanding of others in your life?

    1   2   3   4   5

What type of things will you do to improve your score on expressing love to others?

Total up your spiritual fitness score for all 17 questions:

---

[39]   Webster's, "love."

Interpreting Your Score

Having a spiritual fitness score between 68 and 85 means you have a firm foundation for continually developing your spiritual fitness level. Keep up this commitment level and you will begin to express the fruits of the spirit in your life.

A score between 51 and 67 means that you are well aware of what it takes to develop your spiritual fitness level even further. You sometimes do not follow through on all aspects on a daily basis in order to reach the next level in your spiritual journey. Try to set a goal to increase the daily effort you put into developing your spiritual aspect over the course of the next year.

A score between 34 and 50 means you have experimented with developing these spiritual aspects on an occasional basis. The problem is that you haven't found a consistent plan that can keep you on track to becoming spiritually fit. Try to make time in your life to read your Bible, pray, attend a church, and find a spiritual mentor and you will begin to see results.

A score between 17 and 33 means that you have not made an effort to develop your spiritual fitness. Try to remember that you were created to be a spiritual being and are missing out on a relationship with your creator. Seek a local church or Christian friend that can point you to resources to help in your spiritual journey.

My challenge to all of you is after taking the assessment take some time to write down three goals in the space provided. Then work for one year to develop your spiritual life using the guidelines discussed and keeping in mind the three goals. Then come back after the one year is up and take the assessment again and you will be amazed at your progress in meeting your goals.

S.M.A.R.T. Goals

Goals are specific targets that a person can commit to accomplish in a certain amount of time. They are action-oriented and can help people map out what it is they want to achieve within a certain time frame. There is an easy to use acronym to help write out goals called S.M.A.R.T. This term has many variations but the one we will use stands for Specific, Measurable, Attainable, Relevant, and Time Bound.[40] The purpose of each in terms of writing goals is as follows:

Specific: A goal is specific when you can define it to others in clear and concise terms.

Measurable: The person setting the goal must be able to determine when it is reached.

Attainable: It has to be something that can be reached within the time frame set.

Relevant: It must be important to the individual setting the goal.

Time-Bound: There must be dates assigned to the goal to hold you accountable.

In the space provided below write three S.M.A.R.T. goals that you will set to become more spiritually fit within the next year. Keep these goals handy so that you can refer back to them throughout the time it takes to accomplish them. Then come back at the end of one year and see how you did by taking the assessment again. With the combination of guidelines learned in this chapter and the goals that you write below, one should be on their way to improving their spiritual fitness level. An example of a S.M.A.R.T. goal would be that I will read my Bible for 15 minutes everyday for one year in order to finish the Old and New Testament by December 31st, 2014.

---

[40]   George T. Doran, *There's a S.M.A.R.T. way to write management's goals and objectives.* Management Review 70.11 (Nov. 1981): 35.

1. S.M.A.R.T. goal #1 to work on to become more spiritually fit.

2. S.M.A.R.T. goal #2 to work on to become more spiritually fit.

3. S.M.A.R.T. #3 to work on to become more spiritually fit.

Learning Points from Chapter 2

1) You were created in God's image which includes having a spirit that must be developed throughout your life.
2) We must worship God using our spirit since He is spirit.
3) We were created to have a ruling capacity that allows us to be leaders.
4) Becoming spiritually fit means that you begin to express the nine fruits of the spirit: self control, patience, kindness, goodness, joy, peace, faithfulness, gentleness, and love.
5) The first step to developing your spiritual fitness is to accept Jesus Christ as your personal savior.
6) The second step to developing your spiritual fitness is to utilize the resource of prayer on a daily basis.
7) The third step is to read the Bible daily and apply the teachings in your own life.
8) Find a support system of other Christians that you can learn from in order to develop your own spiritual maturity.
9) Once you have a firm foundation and become more spiritually mature, help others to develop their spiritual maturity level by teaching them some of the things you have learned.

We were created by God to be much more than spiritual beings though. He also created us to be emotional beings as well which leads us to the second aspect that one needs to develop within the holistic approach to becoming a life leader.

Chapter 3

Emotionally Fit

Developing your spiritual fitness level is a good foundation to start with, but it must be balanced with the other aspects to use the holistic approach to become a life leader. Another aspect that is often overlooked by aspiring leaders is becoming emotionally fit. This involves learning to increase your own emotional health level first and then investing in others so they too can develop theirs. In Webster's dictionary the word *emotion* is defined as a strong feeling.[41] These strong feelings are an important part of who you are and are expressed through your relationships with others. They are also considered an integral part of being a life leader because as human beings that were created in God's image man and woman inherited strong feelings from Him. Knowing this, life leaders take into account that both healthy and unhealthy emotions are in their general makeup and focus on nurturing the healthy ones. To learn how to do this you can look to God to see what healthy emotions you have inherited and should be expressing instead of dwelling on unhealthy emotions. Let us now take a look at two stories from the Bible for examples of how the healthy emotions expressed by God can be used to overcome some of the unhealthy emotions that we dwell upon.

For the first story we pick up where we left off with Genesis 2:18. Here we learn that God created a woman to overcome the unhealthy emotion of loneliness expressed by Adam, "Then the Lord God said, it is not good that the man should be alone; I will make him a helper fit

---

[41] Webster's, "emotion."

for him."[42] As the first human Adam was given every kind of creature that was created. Yet having all of these living things was not enough for him as the Bible says in 2:20, "For Adam there was not found a helper fit for him."[43] Like Adam most people find that it is a natural human tendency to express the unhealthy emotion of loneliness that often comes from having a void in their life. As we learned earlier humans are spiritual beings that can only fill their spiritual emptiness with God's love and kindness. It was also because God does express these fruits of the spirit that he loved humans enough to create both man and woman to be together in order to fulfill the unhealthy emotional void caused by loneliness. God is the epitome of relationships; so humans were created in His image to not only worship and have a relationship with Him, but to have a relationship with other humans as well. We are to overcome this unhealthy emotion by embracing our relationships with others.

The second story identifies some healthy emotions that are expressed by God to overcome unhealthy emotions expressed by humans and gives us a clue as to what type of emotions we should continually develop in our lives. In Luke 15:11-32 Jesus tells a story that explains some of God's healthy emotions. The story is actually a parable to explain in simple terms how a complex God operates. The parable is known as *The Prodigal Son* and tells of a father who has two sons. The younger son asks for his share of the father's inheritance and then leaves to "squander" it with "reckless living."[44] The older son meanwhile loyally serves the father and stays by his side never asking for his inheritance. One day the broke and hungry younger son returns to the father with the intent to plead for a job as a hired servant.

Before the story continues it is important to reveal that the father is God and the younger son is one of his people who have chosen a life of sin. The older brother is a faithful follower of God who never chose a life of sin. The rest of the story as told by Jesus will shed some light on the healthy emotions of the father which is really God.

As the younger son is approaching the house the Bible says, "His father saw him and felt compassion, and ran and embraced him and

[42]   Gen. 2.18 (ESV).
[43]   Gen 2.20. (ESV).
[44]   Luke 15.13 (ESV).

kissed him."[45] Here we see that God feels the emotion known as compassion for the returning sinner. The second thing to note is that God embraced him and kissed him which shows the emotion of love. Then the story continues as the younger son says, "Father, I have sinned against heaven and before you. I am no longer worthy to be called your son."[46] The father's reply to this was not harsh words but instructions for his servants to prepare a feast so they could celebrate the lost sons return. The emotion to look at here is that God expresses forgiveness to those who confess their sins, ask to be forgiven, and then turn back to Him. From this we learn that aspiring life leaders who know that they are made in the image of the Father can also reflect the healthy emotion of forgiveness towards those who have done wrong to them and others.

When the celebration was underway the older son heard music and dancing as he came out of the field and drew near to the house. He then became angry after a servant told him what had happened. The father came out of the house and tried to plead with him to join the celebration and be happy. Here we see that the older son showed the unhealthy emotions of anger and resentment towards his father and jealousy of his brother as he said, "Look, these many years I have served you, and I never disobeyed your command, yet you never gave me a young goat that I might celebrate with my friends."[47] The father's reply was, "Son you are always with me, and all that is mine is yours. It was fitting to celebrate and be glad, for this your brother was dead, and is alive; he was lost, and is found."[48]

There are two emotions at play here; the first is sympathy for the older son who is feeling hurt. The second is gladness for the lost son has returned to God after a period of living in sin. The father in this story does a great job of using healthy emotions to manage the unhealthy emotions of his two sons. The lessons from this parable can be used in everyday life whenever a person has to deal with friends, co-workers, or loved ones who express unhealthy emotions. *The Prodigal Son* is just one example but from it we see that God exhibits the healthy emotions

---

[45]   Luke 15.20 (ESV).

[46]   Luke 15.21 (ESV).

[47]   Luke 15.29 (ESV).

[48]   Luke 15.31-32 (ESV).

of compassion, love, forgiveness, happiness, sympathy, and gladness towards His people. While the long time follower of God expresses the unhealthy emotions of anger, resentment, and jealousy. Most people are closer to expressing the unhealthy emotions of the son than they are the healthy emotions of the father. As a person who knows they were created in the image of God, a life leader should learn to express healthy emotions that are similar to those shown by Him in their relationships with others.

To validate this point even further let us turn to another source. A pastor and former Harvard School of Divinity professor named Henri Nouwen who wrote the book, *The Return of the Prodigal Son* which broke down the parable in great detail. When talking about the compassion of the father in the story the author stated the following, "Jesus wants to make it clear that the God of whom He speaks is a God of compassion who joyously welcomes repentant sinners into his house."[49] The author then goes on to state:

> If God is compassionate, then certainly those who love God should be compassionate as well. The God whom Jesus announces and in whose name he acts is the God of compassion, the God who offers himself as example and model for all human behavior. But there is more. Becoming like the heavenly Father is not just one important aspect of Jesus' teaching; it is the very heart of his message.[50]

From this you can learn that you should model your healthy emotions after the heavenly Father. The whole point of Jesus' teaching was to provide examples of how to draw closer to the Father and even become more like Him. By imitating Jesus' teachings and becoming more Christ like, we are actually becoming more like the Father. If God is compassionate to his followers then we should imitate Him and be compassionate to those who follow us and seek help with their emotional

---

[49]   Henri Nouwen, *The Return of The Prodigal Son*, (New York: Doubleday, 1992), 124-125.

[50]   Ibid., 125.

health. The same goes for imitating the other emotions of God such as love, forgiveness, happiness, sympathy, and gladness and using them to help those struggling with unhealthy emotions.

Today we live in a fast paced world that is dominated by consumption which can lead to addictions involving worldly things. These addictions could include: gambling, sex, drugs, alcohol, pornography, food, and even technology. All of them to varying degrees are a result of being emotionally unhealthy. A combination of the way we are raised and how we were created by God contributes to the current emotional level we have. Everyone is raised in a different household and comes from different backgrounds.

The way God created us was to express healthy emotions similar to the ones he expresses in Biblical stories such as *The Prodigal Son.* Yet it is difficult for us to express these healthy emotions towards others because we were raised by parents who struggled with how to express their own emotions towards us. The unhealthy emotions that are manifested from childhood could include anxiety, fear, and anger and lead to addictions or even divorce later on in life. Today those who do get married face a divorce rate of 49.3% according to the National Center for Health Statistics.[51] As an adult every one of us has been given the choice to stop this cycle and express healthy emotions towards others. The important thing is to learn how to improve your own emotional fitness level in order to have better relationships with your spouse and others.

Becoming Emotionally Fit

If we were created to be emotional beings then we must learn how to continually develop this aspect of our lives. There are three steps that are required to go from being unhealthy to healthy within the emotional aspect: build a solid foundation, balance and prioritize your life, and invest in others. The first step is to learn how to build a good emotional foundation to work from. It takes healthy emotions to

---

[51] National Center for Health Statistics, *Marriage and Divorce*, 2008, prepared by the U.S. Dept. of Heath and Human Services (accessed 20 November 2008); available from http://www.cdc.gov/nchs/fastats/divorce.htm; Internet.

overcome unhealthy emotional baggage from your past. Everyone's emotional baggage is different depending on how they were raised. For some of you there is the emotional hole created by a father wound. For others this could be a mother wound that needs to be addressed in order to have better relationships. For an example of this I turn to another personal story in my life.

My father had a mother wound that affected the relationship with his wife and that was passed on to his nine children. I began to realize in my twenties that I harbored this wound inside of me and that I would in turn pass it on to my future wife and children. To break free of this vicious cycle I learned that it took a combination of embracing my spiritual aspect and building a strong foundation using healthy emotions. As we learned from *The Prodigal Son* parable it takes a relationship with God and imitating the life of Christ to learn how to express healthy emotions towards others. The second thing I learned to do was to overcome these angry emotions by using healthy emotions such as forgiveness. Just as God had forgiven me of my sins I had to replicate this forgiveness towards my father for his abuse of my mother. When I had done these two things the transformational results were amazing. The anger within me was replaced with healthy emotions of happiness, gladness, and joy. As I became free from this anger, I was able to concentrate more on improving my relationships with others.

This same format of embracing one's spiritual aspect and building a foundation helped my father as well. He is now 78 years old and has broken his own vicious cycle. He accepted Christ into his life eight years ago and has forgiven his step mother for all her abuse towards him. As a result he is now one of the most loving, compassionate, joyful men I have ever come across. The transformation is like night and day as he witnesses to others about Jesus Christ while expressing these healthy emotions. My hope is that everyone can use this example and learn to accept Christ as their savior and express forgiveness towards those they hold unhealthy emotions towards. This would free up the healthy emotions that God created everyone to express towards others such as compassion, love, forgiveness, happiness, sympathy, and gladness. This definitely is the road less traveled and may take years to fix one's emotional foundation but is a very important step towards becoming a life leader. Once the emotional foundation is set you as an aspiring life leader can then build upon it by following the second step which is to balance and prioritize your life. To demonstrate this I continue where we left off with my personal story.

Fresh off learning how to fix a cracked foundation using healthy emotions I was able to further develop my emotional fitness level by learning how to prioritize my healthy emotions which you can learn from. Shortly after accepting Christ and forgiving my father, I had decided to attend a Christian graduate school called Regent University. While attending the first residency as a doctor of strategic leadership student the director of the program taught us how to balance and prioritize our life. Addressing a group of aspiring leaders Dr. King explained that the order of importance for all decisions we invest in should be God first, family second, work third, and school fourth. This priority list can be used to decide what is major and minor in life, what is worth worrying about, and essentially where our emotional health should be invested. This information proved to be beneficial to a group of busy adults who had church, family, career, and school to balance. Investing in all of these areas in life could lead a person to become emotionally spent very quickly.

A further discussion is needed to learn how to use this priority system to balance where you should expend your emotions in order to remain healthy. The highest priority should always be putting your relationship with God first. With that comes the advantage of allowing God to take on your worries, leaving the path of your life in His hands, and allowing Him to strengthen you emotionally. Faith in God is a powerful way to acknowledge that He has control and that you should not waste emotions on things outside of your control.

The second priority is that of family which should come after God but well before your career. When emotional problems arise you should turn to God first for help through prayer and then to your family. Developing relationships with a spouse and your children should be high on the priority list and where you spend a lot of your time. I also put the category of friends in this section. When faced with an emotional problem a developing life leader should not be afraid to seek counseling from a family member, friend, or pastor who exhibits a higher emotional health level in the area you are struggling with. This allows you to get to the root of the problem of the unhealthy emotions and build upon your healthy emotions. One of the positive things about becoming a life leader is that you will learn to build a strong support system of family, friends, and mentors who can help you to continually develop your emotional health level. For an example of this I turn to another personal story.

As I mentioned before my first marriage ended in divorce. I feel the reasons behind this have a lot to do with the lack of emotional fitness for both parties. Neither one of us had overcome our emotional baggage from how we were raised. While we attended church each Sunday we still did not have a good relationship with Christ. The combination of these two things proved to be too much for us after just two years of marriage. The thing that you can learn from this is that life leaders know how to engage their unhealthy emotions and get to the source rather than just going through daily routines and not working towards a solution to the problem. Digging deeper I found the source of our failed marriage. Like the older sibling in *The Prodigal Son* parable I exhibited anger and resentment towards her as a result of my father wound which made her feel unloved. She too had a father wound which was caused by her dad working three jobs when she was growing up. As a result she was constantly searching for male attention and ended up committing infidelity. After seeking wise counsel I realized that I was biblically allowed the option to let her go. The entire year after this however, was the most difficult in my life emotionally. It was during this period that I put my priority system into place. I first re-established my relationship with Christ and then started attending a church with a 20 something's ministry.

By putting God and the church first I learned how to overcome my father wound with forgiveness. I couldn't have done this if I had my priority list in a different order. As I became stronger emotionally God began to strengthen and form the second priority of family. It was during the 20 something ministry's leadership meetings that I met Kelli. She too had spent the previous year drawing closer to Christ and overcoming past emotional wounds. As we worked together to help other singles in the church we developed a relationship that eventually turned into marriage and the births of three beautiful children. The lesson I learned from all of this was that when we place God first He will help us to establish the rest of our priority system and become emotionally healthy as a result.

The third priority which is a major area in most people's life is that of work. Outside of the relationship we have with God and our family should be the importance placed on balancing emotions at work. Being emotionally unhealthy can cause a lot of stress to be unleashed in the workplace. Using your support network of family, friends, and mentors you should also discuss work issues. Although not as much emotional energy should be spent on this as God and family, nevertheless it is still important to deal with. Having unhealthy emotions that aren't resolved within the first two areas can transfer to the relationships with your boss and co-workers and negatively impact your career. For example the anger and resentment I had towards my first wife translated to my work environment. I was seen as a difficult employee and my career was going no where fast. My career did not improve until I dealt with these unhealthy emotions. For example in my second marriage I have a good relationship with my spouse and the results are amazingly different. By having an emotionally healthy home life I am free to express my healthy emotions of happiness, gladness, and joy to others in the workplace. Finally after all of that your time and efforts can be used to deal with school issues in a similar way if applicable to your life. Once you establish a healthy emotional foundation and a priority system is in place then you can begin to invest in others.

The third step to becoming emotionally fit is to give back to others by investing in their emotional health as a leader. This involves giving support to others as they seek to improve their emotional health level. In fact a life leader is not afraid to use their knowledge and emotional stability to help others at a lower emotional health level. To do this, you must not be condescending but instead have a good relationship with the family members, friends, co-workers, or followers you are investing in. The person receiving the help must see the emotional strength that you have developed in order to feel comfortable in seeking guidance. The key for an aspiring life leader is to practice expressing healthy emotions such as compassion, love, forgiveness, happiness, sympathy, and gladness to everyone. No matter where followers are on their emotional journey it is up to life leaders to be there to help support them. The intent is to allow these followers to surpass you someday on every level. Just make sure that you have developed your own emotional health first as supporting others can drain an emotionally unhealthy person.

One way to help others is through a process called coaching. Coaching is helping another person unlock their potential, transform and grow by asking them powerful questions. The other person you are helping does most of the talking and even might have all of the answers buried deep inside. It is up to us as the coach to ask a series of questions to unlock these answers and then to guide them to write S.M.A.R.T. goals where they can take action to improve in any of the five aspects. We can also serve as their accountability partner or suggest someone who can hold them accountable for achieving their goals and unlocking their full potential.

Coaching is not about us and is all about the person we are helping. You should offer suggestions for improvement only after asking the other person if this is ok. Using powerful questions in all of your one-on-one conversations with someone who comes to you for help is really the basis of coaching and is a beneficial way to develop as a life leader.

Combining the three steps of building a solid foundation, balancing and prioritizing your life, and investing in others should enable you to become emotionally fit and continue your journey towards being a life leader. But first I challenge you to assess your current emotional fitness level and write down ways to improve your score.

Assessing Your Emotional Fitness Level

Rate yourself on the following questions using a scale from one to five. A one means that you currently do not focus on developing that particular aspect in your life. A five means that you are always involved with developing that aspect in your present day life.

1	2	3	4	5
Never	Rarely	Sometimes	Often	Always

Rating: 1-Never to 5-Always (Please Circle)

1. I seek a healthy emotional relationship with God first and foremost in my life.

   1   2   3   4   5

What type of things will you do to make sure that God is first in your life?

2. I seek a healthy emotional relationship with my family as the second highest priority in my life?

   1   2   3   4   5

What type of things will you do to make sure that your family is second in your life?

3. I seek healthy emotional relationships in my career as the third highest priority in my life?

   1   2   3   4   5

Dr. Jonathan Mayhorn

What type of things will you do to make sure that your career is third in your life?

4. I express the emotion of compassion towards others.

      1   2   3   4   5

What type of things will you do to improve your compassion score?

5. I express the emotion of love to everyone I come into contact with.

      1   2   3   4   5

What type of things will you do to improve your score when it comes to expressing love?

6. I express forgiveness to those who have wronged me.

      1   2   3   4   5

What type of things will you do to improve your score when it comes to expressing forgiveness to others?

7. I express happiness or gladness on a daily basis.

      1   2   3   4   5

What type of things will you do to improve your score when it comes to expressing happiness or gladness?

8. I express sympathy for others who need it.

       1   2   3   4   5

What type of things will you do to improve your score when it comes to expressing sympathy?

9. I work towards solving my father or mother wound.

       1   2   3   4   5

What type of things will you do to improve your score when it comes to solving your mother or father wound?

10. I work on having a great relationship with my spouse.

       1   2   3   4   5

What type of things will you do to improve your score when it comes to having a great relationship with your spouse?

Your Total Emotional Fitness Score:

Interpreting Your Score

Having an emotional fitness score between 41 and 50 means you have a firm foundation for continually developing your emotional fitness level. Keep up this commitment level and you will begin to express godly emotions to others.

A score between 31 and 40 means that you are well aware of what it takes to develop your emotional fitness level even further. You sometimes do not follow through on all aspects on a daily basis which is necessary to reach the next level of emotional fitness. Try to set a goal to increase the daily effort you put into developing your emotional aspect over the course of the next year.

A score between 21 and 30 means you have experimented with developing these emotional aspects on an occasional basis. The problem is that you haven't known what to do about your current emotional health. Try to make time to put God first and your family second followed by work or school. Realize that a good relationship at home will aid you outside the home.

A score between 10 and 20 means that you have not made enough effort to develop your emotional fitness. Try to remember that you were created to be an emotional being and are missing out on a healthy relationship with your creator, your spouse, and others. Seek a local church study group, marriage counselor, or books on relationships that can aid you in your emotional journey.

My challenge to all of you is after taking the assessment write down three S.M.A.R.T. goals that you will try to achieve in the next 365 days. Throughout that year work to develop your emotional life using the three step plan discussed. Then come back in one year and take the assessment again and you will be amazed at your progress.

S.M.A.R.T. Goals

Specific: A goal is specific when you can define it to others in clear and concise terms.

Measurable: The person setting the goal must be able to determine when it is reached.

Attainable: It has to be something that can be reached within the time frame set.

Relevant: It must be important to the individual setting the goal.

Time-Bound: There must be dates assigned to the goal to hold you accountable.

In the space provided below write three S.M.A.R.T. goals that you will set to become more emotionally fit within the next year. Keep these goals handy so that you can refer back to them throughout the time it takes to accomplish them. Then come back at the end of one year and see how you did by taking the assessment again. With the combination of guidelines learned in this chapter and the goals that you write below, one should be on their way to improving their emotional fitness level. An example S.M.A.R.T. goal would be, I plan to forgive my father for his treatment of my mother and establish a better relationship with him by June 30, 2014.

1) S.M.A.R.T. goal #1 to work on to become more emotionally fit.

2) S.M.A.R.T. goal #2 to work on to become more emotionally fit.

3) S.M.A.R.T. #3 to work on to become more emotionally fit.

Learning Points from Chapter 3

1) God created man and woman to be together to fulfill the unhealthy emotions of loneliness.

2) We must imitate the healthy emotions of the Father which are: compassion, love, forgiveness, sympathy, happiness, and gladness. We must avoid using unhealthy emotions such as: anger, resentment, and jealousy.

3) A life leader understands that they were created in the image of God so they should use the healthy emotions He has given them to overcome the unhealthy emotions of themselves and others.

4) The way you were raised could contribute to your current unhealthy emotions.

5) The first step to developing your emotional fitness is to build a strong foundation by using healthy emotions to address any father or mother wounds.

6) The second step to developing your emotional fitness is to balance and prioritize your life by placing your emotional energy in the order of importance: God, family, work, school.

7) The third step to becoming emotionally fit is to support others by investing in their emotional health as a leader.

We were created by God to be more than spiritual or emotional beings though. He also created us to have a great mental capacity as well which leads us to the third aspect that one needs to develop within the holistic approach to becoming a life leader.

Chapter 4

Mentally Fit

God created humans to be more than just spiritual or emotional beings, but also to function with a powerful mental capacity. Being made in the image of God allows humans to have a mind that was created by Him. The capabilities of the brain are very difficult for people to grasp because they were made by God who is such a complex thinker. He is in the truest sense a holistic thinker in that He is logical, organized, interpersonal, imaginative, and creative as demonstrated during the formation of the Earth and everything on it. A brain researcher named Ned Herrmann coined the term for the human version of such a complex mind to be known as a Whole Brain®.[52] In this chapter you will find that we have been proven to be able to develop all areas of our mind to become more of a Whole Brain® thinker like God created us to be.[53] You will also discover that a life leader is a person who learns how to become mentally fit which is continually developing their mind in all areas in order to function as a holistic thinker. This approach will benefit those who rely on the life leader to solve problems, make decisions, and look out for their best interest. Before we explore how to become mentally fit we must first learn what it means to not be mentally fit.

A person is not mentally fit when they have given up on the pursuit of wisdom and knowledge. Some people get so caught up in the busyness of life that they let their mind go stagnant and stop challenging it to learn

---

[52]   Ned Herrmann, *The Creative Brain*, revised edition, "Whole Brain®", (Lake Lure: Brain Books Publishing, 1990).

[53]   Ibid.

new things. While reading is one part of challenging the mind it alone is not enough to become mentally fit. Rather you must learn to develop all areas of your brain in order to better serve others as a holistic thinker. God is all about leading people and guiding them using His wisdom. So a life leader realizes this and uses their mind which was created in God's image to seek His wisdom. They then use this wisdom to guide and serve others. To get a better idea of how humans were created to be holistic thinkers in the first place let us take another look at the creation story.

When Adam was first created he was given leadership over every living creature on earth. Once the animals were created God then allowed Adam to name all of them because his intellectual capacity was far superior to theirs. In Genesis it states, "God formed every beast of the field and every bird of the heavens and brought them to the man to see what he would call them. And whatever the man called every living creature that was its name."[54] This job could have easily been left up to God, but was given to Adam because God knew that he was created with a brain that could handle such an important task. However, having leadership capacity as a holistic thinker was taken away from humans when they chose to seek unhealthy knowledge rather then be content with the knowledge the Lord had given them.

At the time there were only two trees in the entire Garden of Eden that were off limits to Adam and Eve. The first was the tree of life which would have allowed them to live forever. The second was the tree of knowledge which would open their eyes to decipher between good and evil. It was Eve who first listened to Satan and ate the fruit from the tree of knowledge because she thought, "the tree was to be desired to make one wise."[55] After Adam and Eve disobeyed God and ate this fruit the Lord said, "Behold, the man has become like one of us in knowing good and evil."[56] As part of their punishment for introducing sin to the world God sent both Adam and Eve out of Eden and from that day forward people would have to work hard for their food. He also punished Eve and all her descendants by making childbirth very painful. Once they were

---

[54] Gen. 2.19 (ESV).

[55] Gen. 3.6 (ESV).

[56] Gen. 3.22 (ESV).

cast out of the garden God placed a guard with a flaming sword at the east gate to protect the tree of life which would have allowed humans to live forever. By disobeying God to seek unhealthy knowledge they caused the rest of us much suffering and a lost chance to only pursue healthy knowledge. This was first evident when having unhealthy knowledge of evil then in turn introduced murder into the world when Adam and Eve's son Cain killed their other son Abel. It wasn't until Jesus died for our sins that we had the most complete tangible example of how to transform our minds to go back to seeking the healthy knowledge we were created to have. To explain the importance of transforming your mind to be ready to become a life leader that functions as a holistic thinker let us turn to another example in scripture.

The apostle Paul was a very knowledgeable scholar on the subject of transformation as he wrote 13 books in the New Testament of the Bible. He learned first hand about transformation because he was once a persecutor of Christ followers even to the point of encouraging their death. It wasn't until Paul had an encounter with the risen Christ on the road to Damascus that he underwent a transformation to become an apostle. The title of *apostle* actually meant that his life mission was to preach the gospel with the authority given to him by Jesus Christ.[57] After this encounter Paul taught others how to transform themselves to become more like Christ who was the image of God on earth. In his letter to the Romans Paul wrote, "Do not be conformed to this world, but be transformed by the renewal of your mind, that by testing you may discern what is the will of God, what is good and acceptable and perfect."[58]

Just as Adam and Eve became content with a worldly pursuit of knowledge so too do we get caught up in similar obsessions while turning our back on the type of mind God meant for us. It is clear that Paul did not want people to be content with the way they were currently focusing their minds. The key phrase to explore further is what Paul meant by "be transformed by the renewal of your mind."[59] There are

---

[57]   Webster's "apostle."

[58]   Rom. 12.2 (ESV).

[59]   Ibid.

three things you must know to help shed light on the purpose of this statement:

1) People must acknowledge who God is in order to clearly perceive Him and his original design for their life.
2) Renewing one's mind is actually the second chance that God gave humans with the new creation which is when Jesus Christ was resurrected. This opportunity for transformation brings with it a new perception of reality that requires humans to have faith in the unseen.
3) The spirit of God is the active agent in the transformation of the mind for those who believe and accept His son Jesus Christ. [60]

Therefore to be a life leader that develops a mind that is more like God requires an entire transformation of oneself through the guidance of the Holy Spirit. After the spiritual transformation is undergone as described in chapter two there is additional work to be done to renew your mind to be one that is in the image of God. This involves stopping yourself from continually pursuing unhealthy knowledge and instead replacing your time with the pursuit of healthy knowledge that is more pleasing to God. This healthy knowledge can be obtained in a systematic way to become a holistic thinker as will be described in the *becoming mentally fit* section.

Scripture is not the only place that supports the fact that humans were created with a far greater capacity for absorbing knowledge and transforming our mind then other living creatures. Scientists have studied this aspect and proved what God originally planned for. The term that is used to describe the different mental processing ability of humans compared to other animals is called cognition. This refers to, "a faculty for the human like processing of information, applying knowledge and changing preferences."[61] The term cognition is also related to concepts

---

[60] Doug Heidebrecht, "The Renewal of Perception: Romans 12:2 and Post Modernity," *Direction Journal* 25, no. 2 (Fall 1996) 54-63.
[61] Science Daily, *Cognition*, (accessed 27 December 2008); available from http://www.sciencedaily.com/articles/c/cognition.htm; Internet.

such as mind, reasoning, perception, intelligence, and learning.[62] At a meeting of the American Association for the Advancement of Science, Harvard professor Marc Hauser presented an article that demonstrates the great rift that exists between human cognition ability and that of animal cognition.[63] He came up with four abilities of humans that make their thoughts unique compared to animals.[64]

1) To combine different types of information and knowledge in order to gain new understanding.
2) To apply the same solution of one problem to an entirely new situation or problem.
3) To create and easily understand computation and sensory images.
4) To detach other modes of thought from these sensory images.[65]

Whether Biblical or scientific based there is no doubt that humans were created with a far greater capacity to learn and absorb knowledge than anything else on earth. It is up to us to spend our time absorbing healthy knowledge that will increase our thinking ability. To become mentally fit as a human is to continually develop the cognitive concepts of learning, applying knowledge, processing of information, and changing preferences throughout your life. Like Adam and Eve we should not store up knowledge that was never intended for us as this may waste time and derail us from becoming a holistic thinker. Now we will focus on what types of knowledge are worth learning to increase your mental fitness as part of the journey to becoming a life leader.

---

[62]   Ibid.
[63]   Harvard University. (2008, February 22). Science Daily, *What Is The Cognitive Rift Between Humans And Other Animals?*(accessed 30 December 2008); available from http://www.sciencedaily.com /releases/2008/02/080217102137. htm; Internet.
[64]   Ibid.
[65]   Ibid.

Becoming Mentally Fit

If humans were created to have the highest level of mental capacity on earth than it is worth discussing how to continually develop this aspect. To think more like God you should work to store up healthy knowledge, expand your mental capacity, and then use your mind to help others. The first step is to store up knowledge by reading and memorizing His words that have been written in the Bible. Paul told his apprentice Timothy that, "All Scripture is breathed out by God and profitable for teaching, for reproof, for correction, and for training in righteousness, that the man of God may be competent, equipped for every good work."[66] Men may have written the books of the Bible but it was God who inspired them with the words He wanted written. Verses in the Bible should not only be read but memorized to store up knowledge which allows you to be mentally competent and ready for any task in life. Doing this daily helps to build up enough knowledge for you to be wise in your leadership of others. Knowledge has been considered power by many since the beginning of time. The Bible helps the aspiring life leader to realize that knowledge should be used to help others rather than to abuse it for power. In fact a life leader is someone who freely passes on knowledge to others without expecting anything in return. Jesus set the example of this when he spent three years passing on knowledge to his twelve disciples without taking anything from them.

Finally, the last benefit of storing up God's word according to Paul is that it allows us to become righteous or free from sin. Unhealthy knowledge can turn into pride which scripture says can be sinful and leads to destruction. Having God's word in your mind allows you to turn away from sin when you are contemplating a temptation in your conscience. This is a vital part of renewing the mind in order to become more of a holistic thinker like God intended all of us to be. In addition to memorizing scripture you should also understand and follow the scientific perspective of improving your mental capacity.

The second step to becoming mentally fit is to understand your own strengths and weaknesses when it comes to your brain's current cognitive or thinking style. Then work to improve the thinking preferences that

---

[66]   Tim. 3.16-17 (ESV).

are weak in order to expand current mental capacity. The reason for this is that a leader can only take their followers as far as they have gone especially in terms of helping them develop their mind. In 1979 Ned Herrmann researched the brain and developed a self-assessment that allowed people to understand their own thinking style preferences.[67] He called this assessment the Herrmann Brain Dominance Instrument© or HBDI©.[68] This assessment lists 120 questions that can be scored and evaluated to provide participants with an understanding of their current thinking preferences.[69] From his research Herrmann concluded that people benefit by knowing how to use a Whole Brain® Model for the purposes of: learning, working, solving problems, and communicating with others that think differently.[70] This Whole Brain® Model breaks up a person's mind into 4 quadrants that show their thinking preferences.

After assessing over 500,000 people Herrmann found that 7 percent have single quadrant dominance; 60 percent have dominance in two quadrants; 30 percent have dominance in three quadrants; and only 3 percent have dominance in all four quadrants.[71] That means that only 3 percent of people were utilizing a whole brain thinking style. We do have the ability to strengthen the quadrants that we are weak in and work towards becoming a Whole Brain® thinker. To improve your mental fitness level as an aspiring life leader you could learn more about how to take the HBDI© to determine your current strengths and weaknesses in terms of preferred thinking styles as found at http://www. herrmannsolutions.com/solutions/. The results are returned in the form of a profile and indicate the degree of preference you would have for each of the four quadrants compared to the other quadrants. Below is a

---

[67]   Herrmann International, "Genesis of the HBDI®," (accessed 3 January 2009); available from http://www.hbdi.com/WholeBrainProductsAndServices/thehbdi.cfm; Internet.

[68]   Ibid.

[69]   Herrmann International, "Overview of the HBDI® Profile Package," (accessed 3 January 2009); available from http://www.hbdi.com/WholeBrainProductsAndServices/thehbdi.cfm; Internet.

[70]   Edward Lumsdaine and Monika Lumsdaine, *Creative Problem Solving: Thinking Skills For A Changing World*, B.J. Clark and Margery Luhrs (New York: McGraw-Hill, Inc, 1995), 79.

[71]   Ibid., 95.

list of the four quadrants and the type of thinking preferences a person uses when they are dominate in that particular thinking style as part of *The four-quadrant Herrmann model of thinking preferences.*[72]

Left Brain Quadrant A thinkers are:
- Logical
- Factual
- Critical
- Technical
- Analytical
- Quantitative.

Left Brain Quadrant B thinkers are:
- Conservative
- Structured
- Sequential
- Organized
- Detailed
- Planned

Right Brain Quadrant C thinkers are:
- Interpersonal
- Kinesthetic
- Emotional
- Spiritual
- Sensory
- Feeling

Right Brain Quadrant D thinkers are:
- Visual
- Holistic
- Intuitive
- Innovative
- Conceptual
- Imaginative

---

[72] Ibid., 81.

The key to remember is to know which quadrants you are currently dominate in and then work to improve upon the one's you are weak in. As you challenge your mind with new things in those weak quadrants you will slowly work your way towards becoming a Whole Brain® thinker. This is important because God created humans to have the mental capabilities of using all four thinking preferences. To give an example of improving weak quadrants in order to later develop followers, I turn to a personal story.

When I was a freshman pursuing a degree in Mechanical Engineering I took the HBDI© as a requirement for a class. My profile scores indicated that quadrant's A and B were my areas of dominance in terms of preferred thinking styles. Quadrants C and D on the other hand scored very low and were my weak areas. After four years of Design Engineering projects that challenged me to be more of a visual, imaginative, and innovative thinker I took the HBDI© again as a Senior. The A and B quadrant scores were still dominate while there was a big improvement in my quadrant D score. After graduating college I spent 8 years as a Design Engineer which improved my quadrant D thinking style even more. That still left me weak in quadrant C thinking because I had never been a very emotional, spiritual, feeling person due to the way I was raised.

My quadrant C thinking started to improve when I began to pursue a renewed relationship with Christ and developed my spiritual side. It also improved when I became married to Kelli who is a very emotional being that taught me to use healthy emotions to replace unhealthy emotions from my childhood. The combination of the two has allowed me to improve upon a very weak thinking area. This brings up another effective way to improve your thinking styles which is to learn from those who are different than you. This shouldn't be limited to friends and family but can include others of different cultures, ethnicities, and backgrounds. Life leaders are those who take opportunities around them to expand their knowledge and expertise. They do this to not only become a better leader but to pass on that expertise to others as well. I have found that learning from different opportunities has allowed me to become a better thinker that can also teach others.

One of the advantages of being strong in all areas of the brain is that creativity is enhanced. Ned Herrmann found that no part of the brain works as creatively on its own as it does when supported by input from the other areas.[73] Having the ability to be more creative can allow you to perform better in your career, hobbies, and in other tasks in life. For example the enhanced creativity has aided my ability to be a better team leader when it comes to projects I work on. By using all four quadrants of my brain over the life of a project I am able to challenge and develop team members' thinking preferences. Therefore life leaders should learn how to improve their weak areas first in order to better understand how to develop the minds of their followers later on.

By taking a look at the four quadrants you should be able to assess which areas you have been dominate in during your life. Then take a deeper look at the weak areas and find ways to use that particular style of thinking more often. Only by challenging the brain to use areas it does not prefer can you truly become more of a Whole Brain® thinker. Combining the two steps of pursuing healthy knowledge and improving upon weak thinking styles should provide a solid foundation for becoming more mentally fit. Remember that life leaders take the opportunities around them to absorb knowledge and expertise and then use it to become a better leader that helps others to do the same. Now I would like to challenge you to assess your current mental fitness level and write down ways to improve your score.

---

[73]   Ibid., 79.

Assessing Your Mental Fitness Level

Rate yourself on the following questions using a scale from one to five. A one means that you currently do not focus on developing that particular aspect in your life. A five means that you are always involved with developing that aspect in your present day life.

1	2	3	4	5
Never	Rarely	Sometimes	Often	Always

Rating: 1-Never to 5-Always (Please Circle)

1. I seek a healthy knowledge by reading and memorizing the Bible?

1   2   3   4   5

What type of things will you do to make sure that you memorize scripture verses?

2. I analyze data and facts to make logical decisions?

1   2   3   4   5

What type of things will you do to make sure that you improve your analytical thinking?

3. I am a detailed person who seeks structure and organization in all areas of my life?

1   2   3   4   5

What type of things will you do to make sure that you have more structure and organization in your life?

4. I plan ahead for things in my life?

       1   2   3   4   5

What type of things will you do to become more of a planner?

5. I a person who communicates well with others?

       1   2   3   4   5

What type of things will you do to improve your score when it comes to communicating?

6. I am a person who can express their feelings to others?

       1   2   3   4   5

What type of things will you do to improve your score when it comes to expressing your feelings to others?

7. I am a visionary who can picture my future life and work towards that?

       1   2   3   4   5

What type of things will you do to improve your ability to be a visionary or future oriented thinker?

8. I am a very imaginative thinker?

       1   2   3   4   5

What type of things will you do to improve your score when it comes to using your imagination?

9. I am a creative thinker?

       1   2   3   4   5

What type of things will you do to improve your score when it comes to being more creative?

Your Mental Fitness Score:

Interpreting Your Score

Having a mental fitness score between 37 and 45 means you have a firm foundation for continually developing your mental fitness level. Keep up this commitment level and you will be a creative person that uses their entire brain.

A score between 28 and 36 means that you are well aware of what it takes to develop your mental fitness level even further. You sometimes do not develop certain areas of the brain or store up healthy knowledge by memorizing God's Word. Try to set a goal to increase the daily effort you put into challenging your brain to improve your weaker thinking styles or memorizing scripture over the course of the next year.

A score between 19 and 27 means you have experimented with developing these mental aspects on an occasional basis but did not have a systematic approach for improving them. Try to make time to memorize scripture and pursue activities that will place you outside of your preferred thinking style. Take up an instrument, foreign language, an art class, or a creative hobby. By challenging your brain in its weak areas you will start to improve them and be on track towards improving your score.

A score between 9 and 18 means that you have not made enough effort to develop your mental fitness. Whether this is because you have been busy with other areas in life or because you didn't want to extend the energy doesn't matter. Try to remember that you were created to be an incredibly intelligent person with untapped potential. Seek books, classes, or discussion group that can challenge you mentally. Find subjects and hobbies that you are interested in and make time over the next year to work them into your schedule. I believe that everyone was created to express the greatness within as long as they work to unleash it.

My challenge to all of you is after you take the assessment write down three S.M.A.R.T. goals that you can work on during the next 365 days. Use the two step plan discussed in this chapter to develop your mental capacity. Then come back in one year and take the assessment again and you will be amazed at your progress.

S.M.A.R.T. Goals

Specific: A goal is specific when you can define it to others in clear and concise terms.

Measurable: The person setting the goal must be able to determine when it is reached.

Attainable: It has to be something that can be reached within the time frame set.

Relevant: It must be important to the individual setting the goal.

Time-Bound: There must be dates assigned to the goal to hold you accountable.

In the space provided below write three S.M.A.R.T. goals that you will set to become more mentally fit within the next year. Keep these goals handy so that you can refer back to them throughout the time it takes to accomplish them. Then come back at the end of one year and see how you did by taking the assessment again. With the combination of guidelines learned in this chapter and the goals that you write below, one should be on their way to improving their mental fitness level. An example S.M.A.R.T. goal would be, to develop my quadrant C thinking preference by taking up lessons on how to play the piano once a week for the rest of 2014.

1) S.M.A.R.T. goal #1 to work on to become more mentally fit.

2) S.M.A.R.T. goal #2 to work on to become more mentally fit.

3) S.M.A.R.T. #3 to work on to become more mentally fit.

Learning Points from Chapter 4

1) We have a mind that was designed by God. We can be holistic thinkers that are: logical, organized, interpersonal, imaginative, and creative.

2) Humans were originally given the highest form of intellectual capacity and thus dominion over other creatures and all the earth until they sought unhealthy knowledge. This brought sin into the world and a more difficult life for all of us.

3) The only way to get back to seeking healthy knowledge is to allow Jesus to transform our minds when we accept the Holy Spirit.

4) The pursuit of unhealthy knowledge must be replaced with the pursuit of healthy knowledge that is more pleasing to God.

5) The first step to developing your mental fitness level is to store up healthy knowledge by memorizing Scripture so that you can be mentally prepared for any situation in life. It should also be used to help others without taking anything from them in return.

6) The second step to developing your mental fitness is to understand your own strengths and weaknesses when it comes to your current thinking styles. Then work to develop the weak areas or quadrants by challenging the brain in the way it thinks.

7) Creativity is expanded when you develop all four quadrants of the brain. This creativity is very useful to help others by solving problems and making decisions.

We were created by God to be more than spiritual, emotional, or mental beings though. He also created us to be physical beings that take care of our bodies, which takes us to the fourth aspect to develop within the holistic approach to becoming a life leader.

Chapter 5

Physically Fit

Today's society has made everyone very aware of the need to get in shape and take care of one's body. Each time you walk through the checkout line at the grocery store or turn on the television, you will most likely see an ad for the latest diet or exercise routine. Yet many of us are still out of shape or overweight and continue to avoid taking care of our bodies which can lead to major health problems. Our being out of shape could be due to multiple reasons that include but are not limited to: no time, not being motivated, and even lack of knowledge on how to go about becoming physically healthy. Being physically fit doesn't mean that you have to spend all your time in a gym bulking up. Instead it simply involves eating healthy and keeping yourself active even if you have limited mobility in order to raise your current fitness level. By discussing the human body from both a biblical and modern perspective I will demonstrate how a life leader continually works towards raising their physical fitness level in order to benefit themselves and others they lead.

From a biblical perspective the Bible has already shown us how God created humans to be spiritual, emotional, and mental beings. It also lays the foundation for taking care of the body as a physical being made in the image of God. From the creation story we learn that God intended to create healthy food for every man and woman to consume. The Lord planted a garden in Eden and out of the ground He made to spring up every tree that was pleasant to the sight and good for food.[74]

---

[74] Gen. 2.9 (ESV).

Then God said to Adam and Eve, "Behold, I have given you every plant yielding seed that is on the face of all the earth, and every tree with seed in its fruit. You shall have them for food."[75] He goes on to tell them that every green plant on earth is to be used for food by all the animals.[76] These verses are important because they show that God created every tree and plant that animals and humans needed to eat to live a healthy life. By allowing the animals to eat green plants from the earth he insured that they would be healthy as well and be ready for humans to eat their meat. The problem is that we now live in a world where processed foods have become convenient for a busy lifestyle. Very few of us today eat fruits, vegetables, and meat that have not been interfered with by pesticides, hormones, or preservatives. Since these foods are no longer in their original form created by God they have lead to most of us having poor diets lacking the nutrients we need. Our society has further discouraged eating healthy by putting such a high price on organic foods that come directly from the earth and are untouched by modern manufacturing processes. Fast food and microwave meals have now replaced God's original method of providing for humans directly from the earth.

The Bible also discusses the importance of taking care of the body beyond just eating healthy food. The apostle Paul taught on the reason why people must take care of their bodies when he addressed the church at Corinth. He states, "Do you not know that your bodies are members of Christ?"[77] He further teaches, "Do you not know that your body is a temple of the Holy Spirit within you, whom you have from God? You are not your own, for you were bought with a price. So glorify God in your body."[78] God did not create the body to watch humans slowly destroy it through neglect. Rather he created their body to house the Holy Spirit he gives to them when they accept His son Jesus Christ. As a way to thank God for giving us forgiveness and the gift of the Holy Spirit, we should take care of our body that houses that gift. Today that means

---

[75] Gen. 1.29 (ESV).
[76] Gen. 1.30 (ESV).
[77] 1 Corinthians 6.16 (ESV).
[78] 1 Corinthians 6.19-20 (ESV).

eating healthy food created by God and exercising regularly. Jesus set the perfect example for us during his time on earth

During his 33 years on earth, Jesus did a lot of walking in order to spread the gospel. Arthur Blessitt is a man who has spent 38 years walking many of the routes Jesus took while carrying a replica of the cross. Using biblical and historical references of events that Jesus participated in, Blessitt has estimated that Jesus walked at least 21,525 miles during his lifetime.[79] To spread the gospel and serve others Jesus had to keep his body in great shape through his eating habits and by walking daily. He couldn't have been as effective of a servant leader if he was overweight or out of shape. Just look at the results of serving the disciples for three years. They ended up founding Christianity which has billions of followers to this day. Therefore life leaders are those who keep themselves physically fit in order to be better prepared to serve those around them. By serving others as a leader one is allowing followers to have the chance to release the greatness within them just as the disciples proved 2000 years ago. In addition to the biblical foundation discussed above there is also medical backing for taking care of your body.

From a medical perspective what does it mean to be physically fit? The Surgeon General from the U.S. Department of Health and Human Services issued a report in 1996 that defined physical fitness as, "a set of attributes that people have or achieve that relates to the ability to perform physical activity." [80] This report outlined the five attributes people must work at to become physically fit:

---

[79] Arthur Blessitt, *How Far Did Jesus and Mary Walk,* The Official Website of Arthur Blessitt (accessed 18 January 2009); available from http://www.blessitt.com/?q=miles_jesus_and_mary_walked; Internet.

[80] U.S. Department of Health and Human Services, Centers for Disease Control and Prevention, National Center for Chronic Disease Prevention and Health Promotion. *Physical activity and health: a report of the Surgeon General.* Atlanta, GA: 1996.

1) Cardio respiratory endurance which is the body's ability to supply fuel during long term physical activity.[81] This means engaging in activities to keep your heart rate up such as walking, bicycling, and swimming.

2) Muscular strength which is the ability of the muscles to exert force during a physical activity.[82] This is means giving the muscles resistance using weights.

3) Muscular endurance which is the ability of the muscle to continue to perform long term without fatigue.[83] This includes activities such as walking, jogging, bicycling, and dancing.

4) Body composition which is the amount of muscle, fat, bone, tendons, and ligaments that make up the bodies overall weight.[84] Not just the weight on the scale but having a healthy percentage of lean muscle compared to the percentage of fat.

5) Flexibility which is the range of motion around the joints.[85] Good flexibility helps to prevent injuries in all stages of life and can be increased with stretching or swimming.

Imagine what you could accomplish if you worked at the above five attributes on a weekly basis. In terms of becoming a life leader you need to continually work at increasing your physical fitness level in order to lead others more effectively. Often followers will respect a leader more if they are in better physical health and take care of their body. Being in shape also allows you to have more energy, better posture, and even more confidence. Followers will notice these things and be influenced and motivated to become more physically active. Now that we know what it means to be physically fit let's take a look at what it means to be physically unfit.

More Americans than ever are either overweight or even obese. According to the Centers for Disease Control and Prevention's 2007

---

[81] Ibid.

[82] Ibid.

[83] Ibid.

[84] Ibid.

[85] Ibid.

statistics, 30% of Americans are obese and 66% are overweight.[86] That means that one third of American adults or just over 60 million are actually at the weight they should be for their height. It should be noted that obesity is defined as having a very high amount of body fat in relation to lean body mass.[87] A person is considered obese if their Body Mass Index (BMI) score is greater than 30.[88] If one has a BMI score between 25 and 29.9 than they are considered to be overweight. A score from 18.5-24.9 is considered to be normal weight while anything below 18.5 is underweight. Anyone can check their BMI score using a calculator found at the Centers for Disease Control and Prevention website: http://www.cdc.gov/nccdphp/dnpa/healthyweight/assessing/bmi/adult_BMI/english_bmi_calculator/bmi_calculator.htm.[89] With just 60 million Americans at the proper weight and even fewer actually working on the five attributes required to be physically fit there is much work to be done. Maintaining a healthy weight can help reduce the risk of having a chronic disease that normally associated with being overweight or obese.[90] So working on your physical fitness allows you to avoid diseases, have more energy, and handle stress better. It is up to you as an aspiring life leader to increase your physical fitness level and then encourage others around you to do the same. The guidelines that follow are intended to help you start on that journey as long as you are cleared for exercise by a doctor.

---

[86] Centers for Disease Control and Prevention, *U.S. Obesity Trends 1985-2007,* prepared by the U.S. Dept. of Heath and Human Services (accessed 17 January 2009); available from http://www.cdc.gov/nccdphp/dnpa/obesity/trend/maps/index.htm; Internet.

[87] Ibid.

[88] Ibid.

[89] Centers for Disease Control and Prevention, *About BMI Calculator:English,* prepared by the U.S. Dept. of Heath and Human Services (accessed 17 January 2009); available from http://www.cdc.gov/nccdphp/dnpa/healthyweight/assessing/bmi/adult_BMI/english_bmi_calculator/bmi_calculator.htm; Internet.

[90] Ibid.

Becoming Physically Fit

To increase your physical fitness level you should learn how to eat healthy and exercise properly. The first step is to change your eating habits to be closer to the way God originally intended. He created every fruit bearing tree and green plant to be a great source of food. Cooking meals daily with fresh fruits and vegetables can give you the nutrients you need. Obviously eating organic fruits and vegetables is better for you as they do not have the pesticides that farmers tend to use. If you can't afford organic products than regular fruits and vegetables are still better than the canned or frozen versions. Also eating meat that is low in fat and grilling or baking it rather than frying it is much better on your digestive system. Food is an important part of preparing your body to have the nutrients and fuel it needs to engage in physical activity.

To lose weight you must speed up your metabolism by eating small meals more frequently. When we eat three larger meals a day there is a drop of energy during mid morning and mid afternoon. The body's metabolism also slows down and burns less calories. To avoid this energy and metabolism drop you should eat between five and seven smaller meals throughout the day. One suggestion is to add a 10:00am and 3pm snack consisting of protein to help fuel the muscles that might be working later that day. This could be in the form of a protein bar or shake and can be found at most grocery or nutrition stores. A rule of thumb for those who are exercising and wanting to lose or maintain their weight is to consume 1 gram of protein for every 1 pound they weigh each day (150lbs = 150 grams of protein/day). For those who want to build muscle and gain weight they should consume 1.5 grams of protein for every 1 pound they weigh each day (150lbs = 225 grams of protein/day). This prepares you for the second step to becoming physically fit which is exercising.

The five attributes required to become physically fit should be worked on each week and fit into your schedule. They include: cardio respiratory endurance, muscular strength, muscular endurance, body composition, and flexibility. To improve your cardio respiratory endurance you need to do activities that keep your heart rate elevated at a safe level for a sustained period of time such as walking, running, bicycling, and swimming. Think of your body's ability to burn calories in terms of a car's ability to burn gas. A driver burns less fuel at steady speeds on the highway and more fuel when they stop and go around town. When you choose to walk or run at a fixed speed and incline level on a treadmill your body is like the car on the highway in that it does not work its hardest to burn calories. Now when you begin to alternate the speed and incline level back and forth on the treadmill your body functions as the car would around town causing more calorie burn. So alternating high intensity and lower intensity cardio should be done for maximum results as long as it is within a safe heart rate as explained below.

When performing cardio respiratory activities you should keep track of your heart rate in order to obtain the best results. Going above the maximum safe heart rate for extended periods of time can overwork your heart and even start to burn muscle. To calculate your maximum safe level heart rate take 220 minus one's age (i.e., 220-30 yrs old is 190 beats/minute). To keep your hear rate at a high intensity level and focus on developing cardio respiratory endurance you should maintain it at .85 times your maximum safe heart rate (i.e., 190 x 0.85 = 161.5 beats/minute). To focus on burning fat you should maintain your heart rate at a lower intensity level of .65 times your maximum safe level (i.e., 190 x 0.65 = 123.5 beats/minute). The second attribute to work on to become physically fit is muscular strength.

The ability of the muscle to exert force during an activity is considered muscular strength. Using free weights or machines provides a resistance that allows the muscles to develop strength over time. Lifting low weight but with high repetitions should be done for those who want their muscles to become toned and do not want to risk an injury. Many men and women prefer this method when starting their work out routines to re-train the muscles and get used to the resistance. Start off by challenging yourself physically by doing 15 to 20 repetitions for 4 sets of low weight. The last 4 or 5 repetitions should burn the muscle and if it doesn't than go up one level in weight. If you can't make it to 15 repetitions then drop the weight one level.

For those who are more advanced or looking to build muscle mass than a higher weight and lower repetition strategy is best. Try lifting heavier weight for 3 sets with 4 to 6 repetitions for each set. The key is to fatigue the muscle on the last 2 repetitions. No matter which method is chosen you should split the muscle groups up based on your busy schedule. Working on 2 muscle groups 3 days a week or 1 muscle group 6 days a week doesn't matter as long as every muscle group is being challenged. Four workouts at the beginner level can be found in the Appendix. Two of them are for working out at home so one is for a man and the other for a woman. The other two are for working out in the gym and also broken up into one for a man and the other for a woman. These workouts were created in consultation with a personal trainer and can be used for up to eight weeks before changing the routine to keep the muscles challenged. The third attribute to work on to become physically fit is muscular endurance.

This involves the ability of the muscle to perform over a longer period of time without fatigue. While weights are used to build muscles, cardiovascular activities can be used to build the endurance of those muscles. Walking, jogging, bicycling, and dancing are all great ways to build muscular endurance. Tying into the cardio respiratory attribute means you should do these activities 2 to 3 times per week for at least 30 minutes. If you are a very busy person then you should try to work on your endurance by taking the stairs instead of an elevator, walking on your lunch break or during the evening around your block. Getting the whole family involved on those walks or bike rides can make the time even more enjoyable while still getting results. The fourth attribute to develop to become physically fit is body composition.

Often people think that the number they see on a scale is the main indicator to managing their weight. Rather it is their body composition that is more important because it tells you how much of your weight is fat and how much of it is lean mass (muscle, bone, tendons, and ligaments). Some of you may have heavier bones and a lower body fat percentage and still weigh more than a person with a higher body fat percentage and lighter bones. It is the person who has a lower percentage of body fat that is considered to be more physically fit. The BMI scale mentioned earlier in this chapter does a good job of gauging whether a person is underweight, at the proper weight, overweight, or obese but it does not measure body fat percentage. Most gyms can measure this or you could purchase a body fat scale using Bioelectrical Impedance

Analysis (BIA) technology. Either way if you are serious about reducing body fat percentage you should have your body composition measured before you start exercising and again a few months later. The final attribute to develop to become physically fit is flexibility.

This involves the range of motion you have around your joints. Developing flexibility can be beneficial because it helps to prevent injuries through all stages of life. As you age you will become less flexible and more prone to injury when doing physical activities. Therefore to become more flexible you should stretch your muscles before and after you exercise. Stretching before a workout allows your muscles to warm up and prevents injury when lifting weights or engaging in cardiovascular activities. Stretching after a workout allows your muscles to cool down and not be as sore or stiff the next day. Other activities to improve flexibility include swimming, martial arts, gymnastics, and dancing. If you don't have time to stretch before or after a workout try to incorporate the above activities into the families' weekly routines to make developing flexibility more fun.

To give you an example of the importance of developing physical fitness and eating healthy I turn to another personal story. In the summer of 2003 I was feeling very weak and out of shape. I couldn't even make it from the car to my desk each morning without being out of breath. At the advice of my co-workers I left work one evening and drove to a clinic to get tested for anemia. When I was signing in and the nurse saw that I wanted to be tested for anemia she took one look at me and said go straight to the emergency room. I did and spent the next 11 days in the hospital being diagnosed with Crohns disease, having some of my small intestines surgically removed, and getting 5 pints of blood. My intestines were slowly bleeding out through my stools until I had such a low blood count that I was on the verge of a heart attack at the age of 26. I had entered the hospital at a weight of 139 lbs and left at a weight of 129 lbs even though I am 5 feet 11 inches tall.

After consulting with a nutritionist I decided to eat healthy foods that would allow my intestines to heal such as fruits, vegetables, and grilled meat rather than fried. I began taking vitamins such as B-complex for energy, iron for red blood cell development, and fish oil for brain function, probiotics to produce good bacteria, and a multivitamin for everything else my intestines couldn't absorb from food. I joined a gym and started toning my muscles with high repetitions and low weights. Drinking protein shakes as my snacks each day combined with working out 4 days a week allowed me to go from 129 lbs to 162 lbs of lean muscle in just 5 months. For the first time in my life I had weighed more than 140 lbs and was physically fit enough to avoid all the medicines that are required to fight the incurable disease known as Crohns which causes the body to attack its own intestines. My doctor's were very amazed and hoped that other patients could follow a similar routine to the one I had developed.

So no matter what you are suffering from physically, eating healthy and exercising can turn things around for you. Once you are physically fit you should work to teach others to do the same as that is one of the major components of the holistic approach to becoming a life leader. Now I would like to challenge you to assess your current physical fitness level and then write down ways to improve your score.

Assessing Your Physical Fitness Level

Rate yourself on the following questions using a scale from one to five. A one means that you currently do not focus on developing that particular aspect in your life. A five means that you are always involved with developing that aspect in your present day life.

1	2	3	4	5
Never	Rarely	Sometimes	Often	Always

Rating: 1-Never to 5-Always (Please Circle)

1. I use fresh fruits and vegetables in my meals?

    1   2   3   4   5

What type of things will you do to make sure that you eat fresh fruits and vegetables more often?

2. I eat 5 to 7 small meals each day to increase my metabolism and energy levels?

    1   2   3   4   5

What type of things will you do to make sure that you eat smaller meals more frequently to keep your energy and metabolism levels up?

3. I take at least 1 gram of protein for every 1 pound of weight each day?

    1   2   3   4   5

What type of things will you do to make sure you get enough protein in your diet each day in order to fuel your muscle growth?

4. I take vitamins and minerals to make up for the nutrients that I am lacking from modern foods?

    1   2   3   4   5

What type of things will you do to make sure you take vitamins and minerals daily?

5. I engage in cardiovascular or muscular endurance activities 2 to 3 times a week?

    1   2   3   4   5

What type of things will you do to improve your score when it comes to engaging in cardiovascular or muscular endurance activities?

6. I engage in strength training by lifting weights at least 3 times per week?

    1   2   3   4   5

What type of things will you do to ensure that you engage in strength training more often?

7. I engage in activities that will improve my flexibility at least 3 times per week?

    1   2   3   4   5

What type of things will you do to improve your score when it comes to developing flexibility more often?

8. I measure my BMI score, weight, and body fat percentage before starting a work out program and at least twice a year after that to gauge my progress?

       1   2   3   4   5

What type of things will you do to ensure that you measure your BMI, weight, and body fat percentage more often?

9. I encourage and teach others around me to eat healthier and become more physically fit?

       1   2   3   4   5

What type of things will you do to improve your score when it comes to helping others to become healthier eaters and more physically fit?

Your Total Physical Fitness Score:

Interpreting Your Score

Having a physical fitness score between 37 and 45 means you have a firm foundation for what it takes to eat healthy and exercise regularly. You also know how to encourage others to be physically fit which is a requirement for becoming a life leader. Keep up this commitment level and you will be a great servant leader that others will want to follow.

A score between 28 and 36 means that you are well aware of what it takes to develop your physical fitness level and establish healthy eating habits. You may not always eat healthy, take vitamins, or protein, or even exercise as often as recommended. Try to set goals for your self over the course of the next year to increase the amount of times each week you exercise and eat healthy meals. Remember it is more than a new year's resolution but rather a lifestyle change that is required to be physically healthy.

A score between 19 and 27 means you have experimented with developing exercising or eating healthy before but have given up and resorted back to your old routines for whatever reason. Maybe you got discouraged, or were not motivated, or didn't know how to go about becoming physically fit. Try to make time to follow the work out programs in the appendix and to shop for healthier fruits, vegetables, low fat meats, and vitamins. By making a lifestyle change you will start to improve your score over the course of the next year and can take the assessment again.

A score between 9 and 18 means that you have not made enough effort to work towards becoming physically fit. Whether this is because you have been busy with work or because you have never been a physically active person doesn't matter. Try to remember that you were created to be a physical being by God and that he intended you to do great things. Try to look at the workouts in the appendix and if you need help ask someone who works out regularly. If you can't work out at home try to join an inexpensive gym and ask for workout advice there. There are also plenty of books, DVD's, and classes on exercising that may help. Try to avoid unhealthy fast food restaurants and processed foods and instead choose healthier foods that are fresh and grilled. There are also many cook books and DVD's that show how to prepare healthier meals.

My challenge to you is after you take the assessment write down three S.M.A.R.T. goals that you can work on during the next 365 days. Use the five attributes discussed in this chapter as well as the exercise routines in the appendix to develop your physical fitness level. Then come back in one year and take the assessment again and you will be amazed at your progress.

S.M.A.R.T. Goals

Specific: A goal is specific when you can define it to others in clear and concise terms.

Measurable: The person setting the goal must be able to determine when it is reached.

Attainable: It has to be something that can be reached within the time frame set.

Relevant: It must be important to the individual setting the goal.

Time-Bound: There must be dates assigned to the goal to hold you accountable.

In the space provided below write three S.M.A.R.T. goals that you will set to become more physically fit within the next year. Keep these goals handy so that you can refer back to them throughout the time it takes to accomplish them. Then come back at the end of one year and see how you did by taking the assessment again. With the combination of guidelines learned in this chapter and the goals that you write below, one should be on their way to improving their physical fitness level. An example of a S.M.A.R.T. goal may be, to lose 15 pounds by July 30th, 2014 through eating healthy and doing a combination of cardio and weight lifting exercises three days a week at the local gym.

1. S.M.A.R.T. goal #1 to work on to become more physically fit.

2. S.M.A.R.T. goal #2 to work on to become more physically fit.

3. S.M.A.R.T. goal #3 to work on to become more physically fit.

Learning Points from Chapter 5

1) God created every plant and animal that we need to use for our food source. The problem is most people get so caught up in their busy life style that they end up eating processed food instead of the healthy food God intended.

2) God created the body to house the Holy Spirit he gives us when we accept Jesus Christ as our savior. We should take care of our bodies because they are to house this gift.

3) Jesus was the perfect example of someone who ate healthy and exercised to take care of the body.

4) The first step to becoming physically fit is to eat healthy foods such as fresh fruit, vegetables, and meat that do not have pesticides, hormones, or preservatives. To lose weight a person should speed up their metabolism by eating 5 to 7 small meals a day instead of 3 larger meals.

5) The second step is to develop the five attributes necessary to be physically fit.

   a. Develop cardio respiratory endurance which comes from engaging in activities that keep your heart rate up such as walking, bicycling, and swimming.

   b. Increase muscular strength by using machines or free weights to provide resistance to the muscles several days a week.

   c. Develop muscular endurance by engaging in activities such as walking, jogging, bicycling, and dancing each week.

   d. Improve body composition by having a healthy percentage of lean muscle compared to the percentage of fat. Use two of your small meals each day to have a protein snack to fuel the lean muscles that are being worked.

   e. Increase flexibility by stretching the muscles before and after exercising or by swimming.

We were created by God to be more than spiritual, emotional, mental, and physical beings though. He also created us to be a relational being which brings us to the fifth and final aspect that one needs to develop within the holistic approach to becoming a life leader. That aspect is to become socially fit in order to be better prepared for the challenges society presents to everyone.

Chapter 6

Socially Fit

God created humans to be more than just spiritual, emotional, mental, and physical beings. He also created them to be social beings that thrive in relationships with other humans. A life leader is a person who understands this and knows how to have a healthy social life that benefits them and their followers as the final part of the holistic approach. They continually develop their social fitness level throughout their life by embracing two different groups of people: those who have similar values to them and those who have a different set of values. A person who does not embrace others and keeps to themselves will never be considered socially fit. However, to demonstrate what it means to be socially fit you must fully understand how God intended us to conduct our social relationships in the first place. This can be done by looking at the very controversial social life of Jesus Christ who was our example of God's perfect image on earth.

During Jesus' first 30 years the Bible gives us stories to demonstrate that He focused on developing His spiritual, emotional, mental, and physical fitness levels. It was not until the last three years of his life and ministry that development of His social fitness level was most evident. The gospels of Matthew, Mark, Luke, and John have many stories that reveal the social life of Jesus at the height of his ministry. From these you will find that Jesus embraced two groups of people during his journey: His inner circle of disciples and the outer circle of people who were very different than Him, but had to be embraced for the greater good of the Kingdom of God. The first group was hand picked by Him while the second group of people came to be involved in His social life at unexpected times.

Looking up the word social you will find that it is defined as, "time that is spent, taken, or enjoyed in the company of one's friends or equals."[91] In the beginning of His ministry Jesus did follow this definition by picking twelve men to live, travel, and work with. From scripture we know that at least four of these men were on a similar level in society in that they were fisherman while Jesus was a carpenter. All twelve became very close friends who looked out for each other and were considered equals in Jesus' eyes. He picked them for both personal and strategic reasons even though they did not know it at the time. While He was on Earth their purpose was to personally support and encourage Him along the journeys. Strategically their purpose was to learn as much as they could from His teachings in order to spread the Gospel after He was gone. As the Bible points out in much of the New Testament, they were successful at fulfilling both purposes.

Just as Jesus demonstrated in picking the twelve disciples, today we too should be comfortable in choosing our close friends to form an inner circle. These friends often share similar values and are there to support and encourage us in good times and bad times. They are the first people we turn to outside of our family when we are dealing with difficult areas of life. In June of 2006 a study was published in the *American Sociological Review* that found the average American had only two close friends.[92] In that same study the percentage of Americans with one close friend was 19 percent while those with no friends made up 25 percent of the population.[93] Not having more than two people in your inner circle can lead to loneliness and even a lack of support structure. To be socially fit as a life leader we must have more than two

[91] *Webster's New Collegiate Dictionary* (1956), s.v. "social."

[92] Miller McPherson and Lynn Smith-Lovin, "Social Isolation in America: Changes in Core Discussion Networks Over Two Decades", *American Sociological Review,* June 2006 [journal on-line]; available from http://74.125. 47.132/search?q=cache:qeOLS1-ZbW0J:www.asanet.org/galleries/default-file/June06ASRFeature.pdf+American+Sociological+Review,+found+25+ percent+of+Americans+do+not+have+a+single+friend&hl=en&ct= clnk&cd=1&gl=us&client=firefox-a; Internet; accessed 21 February 2009.

[93] Ibid.

people in our inner circle as well as embrace a second group of people who do not share the same values and are different from us. This was the controversial part of Jesus' social interactions that we can learn to follow to benefit others we come into contact with. The reason His life was considered controversial was because He embraced people that the "social critics" considered sinners: prostitutes, tax collectors, the disabled, and the sick. Later we will learn that embracing these people as Jesus did is actually a commandment from God.

These "social critics" of Jesus' day were the group known as the Pharisees who followed Jewish law in everything they did. They too believed that the word social meant to only spend time with friends and equals who shared similar values. They considered holiness to be a form of living separate from all of those people who did not share the same values as them. In fact, they were extremely astonished that Jesus was considered to be the "Son of God" by His followers when they thought His miracles were the work of Satan. Therefore, Jesus did not follow their definition of being holy in a social context. Jesus being the divine being that He is had the right to define what being holy really meant in that particular social context and even for us today. Jesus defines holiness as demonstrating perfect love for God and other people.[94] In fact one of the Pharisees who was a lawyer tested Jesus by asking, "Teacher, which is the great commandment in the Law?"[95] Jesus answered him with, "You shall love the Lord your God with all your heart and with all your soul and with all your mind. This is the great and first commandment. And a second is like it: You shall love your neighbor as yourself. On these two commandments depend all the Law and the Prophets."[96] Jesus lived out both commandments because they go together to form healthy social relationships. When you show love to others you are giving love to God as well even if those people are your enemies. After this response the lawyer further questioned Jesus

[94] Jirair Tashjian, "The Social Relationships of Jesus: Discovering Jesus: Part 3", *The Christian Resource Institute*, 13 July 2006, available from http://www.cresourcei.org/jesus3.html; Internet; accessed 10 February 2009.
[95] Matt. 22.36 (ESV).
[96] Matt. 22.37-40 (ESV).

by asking, "And who is my neighbor?"[97] Jesus answered this question using the parable of the Good Samaritan which can be applied to the lives of all who wish to embrace diversity outside of their inner circle.

A Jewish man was traveling the 17 mile journey from Jerusalem to Jericho on a rocky desert path which provided natural cover for some robbers to hide.[98] They came out and stripped the Jewish man and then beat him until he was left half dead. A priest and then a Levite both passed by the victim without stopping to help. What happened next was the Samaritan came down the path and had enough compassion to stop and help the Jewish man. He cleaned up his wounds using oil and wine which were used for healing effects during those times.[99] The Samaritan then put the man onto his own donkey and brought him to an inn where he could take care of him. The next day the Samaritan gave the inn keeper two denarii or the equivalent of two days' wages to take care of the man and even offered to return to cover any additional expenses.[100]

Back then the reason why it was a big deal for a Samaritan to stop and help a Jew was because Jews viewed Samaritans as previous Jews that mixed with pagans from other nations. [101] As a result both groups were very hostile towards one another in public. From a modern social stand point it would be comparable to an Iranian stopping to help a Jewish person from Israel. After telling the parable Jesus then asked the Pharisee, "Which of these three, do you think proved to be a neighbor to the man who fell among the robbers?"[102] The lawyer replied, "The one who showed him mercy." And Jesus said to him, "You go, and do likewise."[103] The neighbor in the second commandment that we are to love and embrace socially is anyone who needs our help. Jesus demonstrated this by embracing all those in need with love and compassion even if they were considered social outcasts by the Pharisees. Just as we are sinners and in no way deserving of God's

---

97 Luke 10.29 (ESV).

98 *NIV Archaeological Study Bible: An Illustrated Walk Through Biblical History and Culture*, (Grand Rapids: Zondervan, 2005), 1691.

99 Ibid, 1691.

100 Luke 10.30-35 (ESV).

101 Ibid, 1691.

102 Luke 10.36 (ESV).

103 Luke 10.37 (ESV).

grace, He still loves us and we can find worth in His love. By the same token the social outcasts that Christ reached out to felt they were loved and had a purpose in life as well.

Jesus went beyond social boundaries and challenged people to think about who should be in their networking groups. So to be socially fit as a life leader means to go beyond current social boundaries that place people into groups based on their values and beliefs. Instead we must embrace diverse people based on who needs our help and show them love and compassion. It is necessary to have an inner circle that supports and encourages the aspiring life leader, but it is also important to continue to develop your social fitness by reaching out to those outside that circle as Jesus demonstrated over 2000 years ago. Throughout His three year ministry He associated with prostitutes, sinners, tax collectors, and the sick who were all considered social outcasts by the Pharisees. He accepted them when no one else would by showing unconditional love. What these diverse people had in common was they needed Jesus' help and had faith in Him as their leader. Today we too can love a diverse group of people even if society looks down upon them. By embracing these individuals we can show what it means to be a socially fit life leader that can help others in need. The following section will serve as a guide for becoming socially fit in today's challenging times.

Becoming Socially Fit

To become socially fit as life leader in modern times you must learn how to associate with two kinds of groups. The first is to make time for friends that share similar values while the second is to make time for individuals that are very diverse in nature. Starting with the first group should be easier since most people gravitate towards others who have similar values, interests, and backgrounds. The advantage of making time for a social inner circle of friends is that you have a support system where you can learn and grow as a person and as a leader.

As an example of this first step to becoming socially fit I turn to another personal story which captures the original group of life leaders. In 2005 I and five other guys would gather on my back porch every evening to discuss leadership. At that particular time these men were my inner circle that I could learn and grow with. They supported and encouraged me as a leader and I did the same for them. These social interactions were a way to challenge each other to do better in all areas of life. If you do not have a strong inner circle of friends then you need to pray and ask God to send this group to you. Then as these people come into your life make time in your schedule each week to meet with them. It could be something as simple as having coffee once a week to discuss what is going on in each other's life. Offer support and encouragement to these friends and they will do the same for you.

As illustrated by Jesus and the disciples this core social group actually prepares us to then minister to the second group that is made up of more diverse individuals. In history other men and women have used a strong inner circle to accomplish God's will such as C.S. Lewis. He was a part of a famous group of writers known as the inklings which met regularly to discuss life as well as the books they were writing. This group went on to write many books on Christianity and were able to touch millions of lives. Social gatherings with your inner circle should be the first step towards growing socially as a leader that will be able to influence others.

The second step to becoming socially fit is to embrace individuals that you come into contact with on a regular basis that have different backgrounds and values. The way to do this is to understand and appreciate diversity just as Jesus did so long ago. If you were to look up the definition of diversity you would find, "a state or an instance of difference."[104] Ask any company today what they think diversity means and they will give you a definition such as the one my current employer gave me when I was hired seventeen years ago, "understanding and embracing differences while using similarities to obtain success."[105] Today the leaders within organizations see diverse people as an advantage because they can bring together many different opinions, ideas, and skills and then turn them into successful initiatives. If leaders of organizations understand this concept very well then why can't a life leader? The answer is they can by learning how to become a person who

---

[104] *Webster's New Collegiate Dictionary* (1956), s.v. "diversity."

[105] Integration, "E-Merger News letter on Diversity," Bellsouth internal private newsletter, (accessed 15 January 2009).

uses the diversity of a social group to bring together great ideas that can help others who are in need. Organizations are not the only examples we have for learning how to embrace diverse groups of people in order to help others as it was also shown by Biblical leaders.

Times have changed as the increased diversity in the world has brought about the term multiculturalism. According to a consulting firm called VISIONS which specializes in multiculturalism, the term means, "a process of change by which we learn to recognize, understand and appreciate our own cultural identities, as well as the similarities and differences of people from other cultural groups."[106] Today most leaders have a diverse group around them. A diverse group makeup refers to how an organization's employees differ in race, sex, and ethnic background.[107] A leader that operates effectively in utilizing its diverse group makeup can be described as a multicultural leader.[108]

Leaders of multicultural followers must work to apply some key principles within the design of their group in order to be successful with diverse followers. One such principle is heterogeneity which implies many different races within a society. All the individuals that make up an outer circle must be seen as a product of a diverse society. Thus diversity must be seen as providing opportunities to be utilized rather than difficulties to be avoided.

The impact of diversity can be drawn from Scripture and applied to those leading others in a social setting. In the letter to the church at Galatia the Apostle Paul talks about treating everyone equal, "There is neither Jew nor Greek, slave nor free, male nor female, for you are all one in Christ Jesus."[109] Here it is recognized that through Christ we are all the same. In today's world we are called as members of Jesus' church to minister His word to all unbelievers and share our love for Him with them as well. Because of his love and grace, we are to extend the same

---

[106] "Multiculturalism". VISIONS, Inc. 23 July 2008.
       <http://www.visions-inc.org/printfriendly/printpage.php>.
[107] Merenvitch, J. & Reigle, D. "Toward a Multicultural Organization". 24 January 2009.
       <http://www.visions-inc.org/articles.htm>.
[108] Ibid, 2009.
[109] Gal. 3.28 (ESV).

to others, regardless of their color or creed. Leading people in a diverse group should be no different because Christian leaders are called to proclaim the power of Christ to others. This calling is not only to be applied to churches, but people in businesses and schools as well. It is not up to us to judge one another based on sex, ethnicity, and race. God loves us all just the same. This is far greater than multiplying clientele base or increasing sales, but reaching a world for God. Our purpose as life leaders should be to reach out and love one another in order to bring others to know Christ especially through leadership roles within a group. This was the whole basis of the second commandment to love your neighbor as yourself even if they are different than you.

Like Jesus, Paul also taught the churches about the second commandment when he referred to treating everyone equally in Romans, "Accept one another then, just as Christ accepted you, in order to bring praise to God."[110] This justifies that as God has accepted us, we are to accept others to glorify Him especially in a social setting and even if it means being uncomfortable. Becoming socially fit has a lot to do with loving, accepting, and helping those who are different than us. This pleases the heavenly Father who created all living creatures whom He loves equally. By loving others the diversity barrier comes down and the chances for successful leadership go up. If given the opportunity to socialize with people different then you take advantage of these opportunities. This could mean sitting with a different group of people during your lunch breaks or joining a social networking group in your city or on line. These encounters may bring you in contact with people from a different culture than you.

An aspiring life leader should also develop the third step in becoming socially fit. That is to learn how to communicate effectively, especially cross-culturally. When communication occurs as a leader, you will be able to accurately convey your ideas and thoughts to those that follow regardless of their cultural background. If followers have no idea what you are trying to convey then your leadership is going to falter. What a life leader must know is that great communicators have an appreciation for positioning their message to be given at the right time and to the right audience, because they understand the various

---

[110] Rom. 15.7 (ESV).

people they are trying to reach and what they can and can't hear. You must send your message in through an open door rather than trying to push it through a wall. Everyone's behavior, actions, and decisions are considered communication so you as a leader have to learn how to create a consistent message through these.[111]

A leader that does not take the time to learn how their actions, facial expressions, and behaviors are perceived in another culture can also be set up for failure. For example, when the elder President George H. Bush was speaking in Australia he used his index and middle finger to form a "V" for victory. What he didn't know is that this is the equivalent of the middle finger in America. Therefore take the time to understand followers of other cultures before communicating your message. Jesus did this best by first listening to those who were rejected by society and then conveying his consistent message to them.

I have been teaching two classes part time each semester in an Engineering program at a major University for four years now. There are five different classes that I teach on topics such as process improvement, project management, and leadership. In every class I always make time in the semester to teach the students how to build and lead powerful diverse teams. This benefits them in the four year Engineering program because they work on team projects in all of their classes. But more importantly, it will benefit them for the rest of their career because they will have to work in diverse teams as industry is now more global than ever. Look around you next time you go to work, school, church, or even the mall and you will see how diverse society has become. It requires us to improve our skills as a multicultural life leader who can use that diversity to benefit our followers.

Regardless of how healthy your current social life is you can work on improving your fitness level in this area. Having a great inner circle to support and allow you as an aspiring life leader to grow is the first step. The second is to be surrounded by a diverse group of individuals that can interact with you and in turn help each other to grow. All the different opinions, ideas, and values that surface can be

[111] Harvard Business School. *What Makes a Good Leader* (accessed 20 June 2007); available from http://hbswk.hbs.edu/item.jhtml?id=2141&t=leadership&noseek=one; Internet.

combined for the greater good of the social group. Finally, learn how to communicate with a group of people who are from a different culture than you as the leader. Learn about the other cultures and understand their communication style before resorting to the verbal and nonverbal forms of communication prevalent in your own country. Now I would like to challenge you to assess your current social fitness level and then write down ways to improve your score. Then come back in one year and take the assessment again to see how much your social fitness level has increased.

Assessing Your Social Fitness Level

Rate yourself on the following questions using a scale from one to five. A one means that you currently do not focus on developing that particular aspect in your life. A five means that you are always involved with developing that aspect in your present day life.

1	2	3	4	5
Never	Rarely	Sometimes	Often	Always

Rating: 1-Never to 5-Always (Please Circle)

1. I consistently have 3 to 5 friends who I can call upon to be my inner circle?

   1   2   3   4   5

If you do not have this many friends in your inner circle on a consistent basis what will you do to find more?

2. I make time to spend with my inner circle of friends?

   1   2   3   4   5

What type of things will you do to make sure that you spend more time each week with your close inner circle of friends?

3. I use my social time with my inner circle of friends wisely so that I am growing as a person?

   1   2   3   4   5

What type of things will you do to make sure that your inner circle of friends challenges you to grow as a person and life leader?

4. I make time to spend with a very diverse group of people outside my inner circle of friends?

    1   2   3   4   5

What type of things will you do to make sure you spend more time with a diverse group of people?

5. I use the time that I spend with a diverse group of people wisely so that I grow as a person?

    1   2   3   4   5

What type of things will you do to make sure that you grow as a person in a diverse group setting?

6. I embrace the ideas, opinions, and values of diverse individuals in order to help others?

    1   2   3   4   5

What type of things will you do to improve your score when it comes to embracing the ideas, opinions, and values of diverse individuals in order to help others?

7. I make time to learn about people from a different culture?

    1   2   3   4   5

What type of things will you do to learn more about people from different cultures than you?

8. I am an active listener to those from a different culture or background than me?

      1   2   3   4   5

What type of things will you do to improve your score when it comes becoming a better listener to those who are different than you?

9. I am an effective communicator in a social setting in that I can use my verbal and nonverbal language to help others in need?

      1   2   3   4   5

What type of things will you do to ensure that you become a great communicator that can help others with your verbal and non verbal language?

Your Total Social Fitness Score:

Interpreting Your Score

Having a social fitness score between 37 and 45 means you have a firm foundation for what it takes to embrace different groups of people in your social life. You also know how to help others through your social networking groups which is a major requirement for becoming a life leader. Keep up the regular effort required to embrace these various groups of people and your followers will benefit greatly.

A score between 29 and 36 means that you are well aware of what it takes to develop your social fitness level and embrace different groups of people. You may not always make time to socialize with diverse people or have your inner circle there for support. Try to set goals for your self over the course of the next year to increase the time spent each week with interacting with an inner circle and a diverse group of people.

A score between 21 and 28 means you have tried to have a healthy social life before but are not very consistent in developing this area of your life. Try to look around and find an inner circle of friends that you can trust and spend time with. Use their support to grow as a person and as a leader. Then look beyond this group for some diverse people at your work, church, school, or hobbies and spend time with them. Learn from them and leverage their differences to help others. By making more time to spend with these groups you will start to improve your score over the course of the next year and can then take the assessment again.

A score between 13 and 20 means that you have not made enough effort to work towards becoming socially fit. This might mean that you spend a lot of time you're your family or at work and do not make time for a social life. Remember the advantages of taking a break and learning to grow by talking to others. Also, having diverse people can expand your leadership skills as well as help others in need. Learn how to listen to people with different values, opinions, ideas, and even from a different culture. Practice communicating with others and note how effective you are in your expression of verbal and nonverbal language. Try to remember that you were created to be a social being by God and that he intended you to love others just as He loves you. Once you love others they barriers of diversity will come down and those differences will be leveraged as similarities for the greater good of the group.

My challenge to you is after you take the assessment write down three S.M.A.R.T. goals that you can work on during the next 365 days. Use the three steps discussed in this chapter as well as these goals to develop your social fitness level. Then come back in one year and take the assessment again and you will be amazed at your progress.

S.M.A.R.T. Goals

Specific: A goal is specific when you can define it to others in clear and concise terms.

Measurable: The person setting the goal must be able to determine when it is reached.

Attainable: It has to be something that can be reached within the time frame set.

Relevant: It must be important to the individual setting the goal.

Time-Bound: There must be dates assigned to the goal to hold you accountable.

In the space provided below write three S.M.A.R.T. goals that you will set to become more socially fit within the next year. Keep these goals handy so that you can refer back to them throughout the time it takes to accomplish them. Then come back at the end of one year and see how you did by taking the assessment again. With the combination of guidelines learned in this chapter and the goals that you write below, one should be on their way to improving their social fitness level. An example of a S.M.A.R.T. goal would be, to form an inner circle of three friends that discuss life at least 3 times per week during lunch in the work cafeteria starting April of 2014.

1) S.M.A.R.T. goal #1 to work on to become more socially fit.

2) S.M.A.R.T. goal #2 to work on to become more socially fit.

3) S.M.A.R.T. goal #3 to work on to become more socially fit.

Learning Points from Chapter 6

1) Jesus surrounded himself with two groups of people: an inner circle made up of twelve disciples that had similar values and a second group of people who were considered diverse or social outcasts.

2) Jesus taught us to live out the two greatest commandments in our social lives. The first is to love the Lord your God with all your heart and the second is to love your neighbor as yourself. A neighbor is anyone who needs your help even if they are different from you.

3) The first step to becoming socially fit is to embrace your inner group of friends in order to become strengthened and supported as a leader.

4) The second step to becoming socially fit is to embrace a second group of people that are very diverse in nature. You can learn from these people and leverage their strengths for the good of the group and to help others in need.

5) The third step to becoming socially fit is to learn to communicate effectively, even cross culturally. To do this you have to learn to listen to others and work on your own methods of sending the right message no matter the culture of the recipients.

Up to this point we have discussed how humans were created by God to be spiritual, emotional, mental, physical, and social beings. Now it is time to discuss how to use all of these aspects as a cohesive unit in order to become totally fit as a life leader that others want to follow.

Chapter 7

Totally Fit

The five individual parts of the holistic approach have been discussed in great detail, but now it is time to see why it is important for them to be developed together. As mentioned in chapter one all five are interdependent parts that make up the whole person. No individual should just develop a single aspect while leaving the other four undeveloped. Instead an aspiring life leader is someone who develops all five areas on a daily basis. With busy lifestyles this means using effective time management to develop some of the areas at the same time. The way to do this is to realize that these aspects mesh well together in everyday life and then look for situations to develop them simultaneously. The end result for the hard work put into developing all aspects is becoming a totally fit individual that is ready to be a life leader.

The key term to remember to understand the power of the holistic approach is that developing all aspects together produces synergism. There are two definitions of synergism found in the dictionary; the first has a physiological basis, "cooperative action of discrete agencies such that the total effect is greater than the sum of the effects taken independently."[112] The second has a theological basis, "the doctrine that in regeneration [being reborn spiritually] there is a co-operation of divine grace and human activity."[113] Both definitions help to explain how combining the development of the human aspects (mental, physical, and social) with the divine influenced aspects (emotional and spiritual)

---

[112] Webster's "synergism."

[113] Ibid, 862.

can allow us to be more effective than developing any one part by itself. Before you can use the holistic approach effectively as a life leader you must first learn why it is important to develop these aspects together.

Any one aspect and its relationship to the others can be analyzed to show why they all should be developed together. Take the spiritual aspect, which was discussed first because it requires faith in our Creator and forms a basis for all of the other aspects described in this book. When you are working on developing your spirituality you should also be able to easily develop your emotional, mental, physical, and social aspects. Let us start with how spending time developing your spiritual fitness can also lead to increased emotional health.

Reading the Bible, praying, worshipping, and seeking spiritual mentorship all contribute to developing a stronger faith in God. As that faith increases it leads to the transformation of our hearts with the filling of the Holy Spirit. This in turn leads to the expression of the Fruits of the Spirit: self control, patience, kindness, goodness, joy, peace, faithfulness, gentleness, and love. These Fruits of the Spirit bring with them a set of healthier emotions that replace the Fruits of the Flesh which contain or are caused by unhealthy emotions. Just look at the Fruits of the Flesh as mentioned by the Apostle Paul: sexual immorality, impurity, sensuality, idolatry, sorcery, enmity, strife, jealousy, fits of anger, rivalries, dissensions, divisions, envy, drunkenness, and orgies.[114] Some of these are unhealthy emotions such as anger, jealousy, and envy. Others are caused by unhealthy emotions inside of us such as drunkenness, sexual immorality, and rivalries. When we allow the Holy Spirit to transform us during our spiritual development we can replace those unhealthy emotions with good emotions such as: joy, peace, and love. Our healthy emotions also cause better actions as shown by these Fruits of the Spirit: self-control, patience, kindness, goodness, and gentleness. When you develop your spiritual fitness you are not only developing your emotional aspect but your mental fitness as well.

According to a 2008 Missouri University study there is evidence that spiritual experiences are related to decreased activity in the right

---

[114] Gal. 5.19-21. (ESV).

side of the brain.[115] The study focused on people who had injuries to the right parietal lobe of the brain which resulted in lower functioning activity in that area. The researchers found that individuals with these injuries had higher reported levels of spiritual experiences such as selflessness and transcendence.[116] What this proves is that putting the needs of others before you is a spiritual benefit that can be developed by decreasing activity in the right parietal lobe of the brain. To decrease this activity in that side of the brain a person simply needs to use prayer or meditation according to the study.[117] The researchers also found that people who use prayer to reduce activity on the right side of the brain are considered more mentally healthy especially if they have a positive belief that there is a God who loves them.[118] This is a great example of how when you develop a closer relationship with God and become more spiritually fit you are also developing your mental fitness at the same time. Developing spirituality also increases our physical fitness levels.

When the Apostle Paul was teaching his young apprentice Timothy about being a good leader he expressed the importance of developing not only physical fitness but also spiritual fitness. Paul wrote, "train yourself for godliness; for while bodily training is of some value, godliness is of value in every way, as it holds promise for the present life and also for the life to come. The saying is trustworthy and deserving of full acceptance."[119] Paul was acknowledging that physical fitness is necessary but even more important is spiritual fitness because it helps now and after people have gone on to Heaven. The reason why physical fitness can be developed more easily when you develop spiritual fitness is because God created the body to house the Spirit. When the Spirit is developed inside of the body then you can rely on God to help develop that body. For example, when someone struggles with health or weight issues they can use the resource of prayer to ask God to be the center

---

[115] University of Missouri-Columbia. *Selflessness -- Core Of All Major World Religions -- Has Neuropsychological Connection.* Science Daily, (accessed 27 December 2008); Available from http://www.sciencedaily.com /releases/2008/12/081217124156.htm; Internet.

[116] Ibid.

[117] Ibid.

[118] Ibid.

[119] 1 Tim. 4.7-9 (ESV).

of their physical development. Within their prayers they can ask for strength, encouragement, and even a support system that will help them become physically healthy. Faith in God also gives us hope and a positive attitude in order to get through challenges we may face on our way to becoming physically fit. Last but not least developing spiritual fitness can also help improve social fitness.

In the course of developing spiritual fitness you will need to reach out to other Christians for guidance and fellowship. This could be in the form of small groups at a local church or from other believers at your workplace or school. These inner support networks that are needed to grow spiritually also provide a way to grow socially. Faith and religion are not going to be the only things discussed in these groups. Rather the topics will vary tremendously and deal with areas such as life, love, and careers. To give you an example of this I turn to another personal story. The two twenty-something ministries I have led always started out with a biblical lesson but ended up talking about everyday topics that the group was dealing with. Recognizing this I always tried to find a way to tie spiritual and social fitness together in the discussions so that participants could grow in both areas.

The above relationships between developing spiritual fitness and the other aspects show just one set of combinations possible. We could have discussed many more combinations of how all the aspects can be improved together but will save some additional examples for the section below. The reason why they all should be developed simultaneously is because they were designed by our Creator to be used together. Keep in mind that the result of obtaining a high level of fitness in all areas is that it produces synergism. This synergy is what makes the holistic approach to becoming a life leader so effective. Becoming totally fit is easier said than done with today's demanding schedules. So now it is time to show how to manage the weekly routine necessary to develop all aspects.

Making Time to Become Totally Fit

The biggest push back for accepting the holistic model to becoming a life leader will be from people who say they don't have the time. Every one of us has the same amount of time in a day yet life leaders are those who take the initiative to make time for the things that matter. Going back to the emotional chapter it is about repairing your foundation and prioritizing your life to spend time and energy in the right places. People should remember the order of importance for things in life: God, family, health, work, school, and social activities. I have added health and social activities to the sequence to help you make the right decisions when it comes to managing the time required to become totally fit.

At the end of the chapter I have provided two schedules for becoming totally fit. The first is an example of my own schedule during the busiest part of my development. The second has empty slots for you to start filling out your weekly schedule in order to make time to develop all five areas. The first thing you should do is block off the most important thing which is developing a close relationship with God in the form of spiritual development. This time should be non-negotiable and everyone in your life needs to respect that. This will include the time it takes to go to church on Sundays and/or Wednesdays. It will also include any small groups or Bible studies you become a part of that meet on a weekly basis. Then schedule a quiet time for at least twenty minutes each day to read your Bible, pray, and listen to God. For some of you this will be first thing in the morning, at lunch, or after the kids go to bed at night. Finally make time to develop others' spiritual fitness by mentoring them on what you have learned that might help. The second most important focus in everyone's life should be on their family.

Periods of time on the schedule need to be blocked off for developing healthy emotional connections to your family. First and foremost should be quality time set aside to spend with a spouse. This could include activities such as: eating dinner, talking, and walking. Then additional time should be set on the schedule for giving attention to kids or other family members. After you have a fixed schedule for spending uninterrupted time with your family you can then focus on developing others emotional fitness. Part of being a life leader is to serve others without expecting anything in return. This is true in the emotional aspect and involves making time for helping friends overcome unhealthy feelings or father/mother wounds. Blocking off time to listen to these friends can really help their development and also serve as a social development for you. The third category that we should make time for is our health.

In the physical fitness chapter we learned about the importance of eating healthy and exercising. Both require a lot of time to be set aside within the schedule so that other non essential activities do not keep us from engaging in physical development. Eating healthy requires extra time each evening to prepare and cook fresh food for dinner or for lunch the next day. If time isn't blocked off to make this a daily habit then fast food stops will take over again and break the healthy diet. Also, the frequent smaller meals or protein snacks need to be scheduled in during the mid morning and mid afternoon times to speed up the metabolism and feed the developing muscles. Your schedule should also leave time for developing cardio respiratory endurance, muscular strength, and flexibility. Take a look at the four work outs I have included in the Appendix if you need some routines to start with for the first six to eight weeks. Try to schedule an hour each day for three days a week at first. Then work up to four and eventually five days a week as your muscles get used to the exercises. You may be able to save some time by combining your exercises with your social development by having a workout partner to support you. The next major item to focus on is developing at work.

Most people have to spend at least forty hours each week on their job. This is a large block of the schedule that can't be adjusted. Yet a life leader is someone who finds ways to develop holistically even at work. This could include taking your lunch breaks at the same time as your inner circle of co-workers. The emotional and social development that takes place five days a week during lunch can be powerful. Also, this time could be used to develop an outer circle of friends that are very diverse. We can learn a lot from people who we normally do not hang out with on a daily basis. Both groups could also use your help, as a life leader always looks for ways to give back to others. Mental development can happen at work as well if there are classes or training programs offered to you. When given the chance to learn new things outside of your normal work duties make time for them. Some of my best mental development has come from leadership courses offered at work. The next category to keep in mind when filling out your schedule is school or continual learning.

Even if you are done with school you should never stop taking new classes or training programs which is what I call being a life-long learner. To develop all four areas of the brain we must continually challenge it by learning new things. For some this will be going back to school and for others this will be reading and writing things that challenge them. Whichever avenue you choose does not matter as long as you are continually learning. Don't forget to make time for some creative brain development such as art classes, musical instruments, or other hobbies. Go ahead and block this time off as soon as you can before you go onto the last aspect of making time for social activities.

Developing your social fitness can be combined with the other four aspects in the holistic approach. Yet, for some people this development can be either non existent or overdone. The reason why I want you to schedule this last is because the other aspects need time set aside first. Some people will get their social development already and others will need to block off a set amount of time. I know that developing the other four aspects do provide some social development for all of us. But blocking off specific time for social activities allows us to say no to other people who could easily fill that time up. For example, every Thursday night from 7pm to 9pm is reserved for a close friend and I to have dinner and talk. Although this time is marked for social development at times it has taken on spiritual development in the form of Bible studies. Some weeks the focus is on mental development in the form of a book study or emotional development in the form of discussing relationships. So be sure and block off some time each week for social development.

This should conclude all the major items needed to make time to become totally fit. Take a look at the remaining blank time slots on your schedule. These times are reserved for all of the other things in life that you enjoy such as: watching TV, sleeping, and relaxing. The point of this section was to show you that when you prioritize your life into a schedule you can make time to accomplish what is necessary to become totally fit. You may have to give up non essentials such as certain television programs or excessive social activities to make this work. The benefits of developing every area will far outweigh the things you will be giving up. Following your new schedule consistently will put you in the minority of people and that is why I call it the road less traveled. On the next few pages you will find an example of my schedule followed by a blank schedule for you to fill out to become totally fit.

Now it is time to discuss how the holistic approach in this book can tie into your life. No matter what your current situation is the next chapter will help you apply life leadership to improve it. You will find out how to combine your passions and total fitness to unleash the greatness within. My challenge to you is to read on to learn more about the benefits of becoming a life leader.

Jonathan Mayhorn's Example Schedule Used to Become Totally Fit

Time	Monday	Tuesday	Wednesday	Thursday	Friday	Saturday	Sunday
5:00am	Ready	Ready	Ready	Ready	Ready	Sleep	Sleep
5:30am	Drive	Drive	Drive	Drive	Drive	Sleep	Sleep
6:00am	Run	Run	Run	Run	Run	Sleep	Sleep
6:30am	Weights	Weights	Weights	Weights	Weights	Sleep	Sleep
7:00am	Bible	Bible	Bible	Bible	Bible	Bible	Bible
7:30am	Breakfast	Breakfast	Breakfast	Breakfast	Breakfast	Ready	Ready
8:00am	Teach	Teach	Teach	Teach	Teach	Breakfast	Breakfast
8:30am	Teach	Teach	Teach	Teach	Teach	TV	Drive
9:00am	Work	Work	Work	Work	Work	Read	Small Groups
9:30am	Work	Work	Work	Work	Work	Read	Small Groups
10:00am	Protein	Protein	Protein	Protein	Protein	Protein	Church
10:30am	Work	Work	Work	Work	Work	Relax	Church
11:00am	Work	Work	Work	Work	Work	Weights	Drive
11:30am	Work	Work	Work	Work	Work	Cardio	Relax
12:00pm	Lunch	Lunch	Lunch	Lunch	Lunch	Lunch	Lunch
12:30pm	Lunch	Lunch	Lunch	Lunch	Lunch	Lunch	Lunch
1:00pm	Work	Work	Work	Work	Work	Family	Family
1:30pm	Work	Work	Work	Work	Work	Family	Family
2:00pm	Work	Work	Work	Work	Work	Friends	Friends
2:30pm	Work	Work	Work	Work	Work	Friends	Friends
3:00pm	Protein	Protein	Protein	Protein	Protein	Protein	Protein
3:30pm	Work	Work	Work	Work	Work	Relax	Relax
4:00pm	Drive	Drive	Drive	Drive	Drive	Grade Papers	Grade Papers
4:30pm	Drive	Drive	Drive	Drive	Drive	Grade Papers	Grade Papers
5:00pm	Family	Family	Family	Family	Family	Grade Papers	Grade Papers
5:30pm	Family	Family	Family	Family	Family	Homework	Homework
6:00pm	Dinner	Dinner	Dinner	Dinner	Dinner	Dinner	Church
6:30pm	Dinner	Dinner	Dinner	Dinner	Dinner	Dinner	Church
7:00pm	Family	Family	Family	Social	Family	Family	Dinner
7:30pm	Family	Family	Family	Social	Family	Family	Dinner
8:00pm	Family	Family	Family	Social	Family	Family	Family
8:30pm	Family	Family	Family	Family	Family	Family	Family
9:00pm	Reading	Reading	Reading	Reading	Reading	Reading	Reading

Blank Schedule to Use to Become Totally Fit

Time	Monday	Tuesday	Wednesday	Thursday	Friday	Saturday	Sunday
5:00am							
5:30am							
6:00am							
6:30am							
7:00am							
7:30am							
8:00am							
8:30am							
9:00am							
9:30am							
10:00am							
10:30am							
11:00am							
11:30am							
12:00pm							
12:30pm							
1:00pm							
1:30pm							
2:00pm							
2:30pm							
3:00pm							
3:30pm							
4:00pm							
4:30pm							
5:00pm							
5:30pm							
6:00pm							
6:30pm							
7:00pm							
7:30pm							
8:00pm							
8:30pm							
9:00pm							

Learning Points from Chapter 7

1) Developing all aspects together is powerful because it produces synergism.

2) Synergism allows us to be more effective as a life leader by combining the development of the human aspects (mental, physical, and social) with the divine influenced aspects (emotional and spiritual).

3) The various parts can be developed simultaneously because God created them to be used together.

4) Developing the aspects together also saves more time then developing them individually.

5) To become totally fit you must use effective time management by creating a schedule. To do this you must know the order of importance when it comes to blocking off time for development activities. The order you should use to fill out the schedule is: God, family, health, work, school, and social activities. After all of the development areas are marked on your schedule you can use the rest of the time slots for relaxing, sleeping, and other activities.

6) Use the sample schedule I use to become totally fit on the previous pages as a guide to fill out the blank schedule for your life.

Chapter 8

Application to Your Life

Up until this point we have covered how to become spiritually, emotionally, mentally, physically, and socially fit. We have also learned how to manage our time in order to develop these aspects together to become totally fit. So where do you go from here? To answer this I would like to explain how all of this will apply to your life regardless of who you are or what you do. I will discuss how to find your passion and what it has to do with becoming totally fit. Then I will lay out what a life leader is and give different principles that a life leader can live by. Finally I will challenge you to become a life leader others want to follow.

In the previous chapter you should have learned how total fitness is the result of developing all five aspects. Becoming totally fit gives you the necessary training required to use the holistic approach to become a leader in your life. After having spent so much time developing the holistic approach you need to know where to apply it within your life. Using it everywhere will burn you out and never produce the results you are looking for. Instead everyone needs to find the greatness with in and use it to be an effective life leader. The greatness within you is a combination of your passion and becoming totally fit. Finding your passion and developing all aspects of the holistic approach will allow you to be a very effective life leader.

Passion + Total Fitness = Finding the Greatness Within
Finding the Greatness Within = Effective Life Leader

Passion is one of those terms that people use a lot but do not know how to apply to their life. To find your passion in life you must know what it truly means. The best definition I have ever heard was spoken by Bill Hybels, the Senior Pastor of Willow Creek Community Church, at a leadership summit. Hybels defined passion as, "something you can't stand in life but have to do something about."[120] This should be something that burns inside of you so much that you get frustrated because you want to throw all of your skills, gifts, and efforts toward it. For example, I have never been able to stand poor leaders. When I came out of engineering school and started my career at a fortune 100 company, I had expected most of the managers to know how to be good leaders. Instead I found that they did not know how to lead effectively. At first this was very frustrating, but finally I realized that I had to do something about it. I set out to gain the skills necessary to teach others how to be great leaders by going back to school for a Masters in Engineering Management. When this didn't give me all the skills I needed to pursue my passion, I went back to school for a Doctorate in Strategic Leadership while continually applying what I was learning towards teaching others how to be effective leaders in their own life. So ask yourself, "What is it you can't stand the most in life but have to do something about?" Answering this question will help you to find the passion that lies deep inside of you.

This passion was given to you by God Himself and is your calling in life. Once you know what this is you have to develop the right tools to pursue this calling. Those tools are also given to you by God and are the five aspects that you must improve to be totally fit. Therefore combining your God given passion with the fully developed aspects of the holistic approach will unleash the greatness God created within you. So an effective life leader is someone that uses the holistic approach to pursue their passion. As you do this you will find that others will follow that passion. It is up to you as a life leader to help these followers develop their total fitness levels and to find their own passion. I challenge you to start thinking about what your passion is as you are developing the five aspects to become totally fit. Then when you become totally fit you

---

[120] Bill Hybels, *Passion,* The Leadership Summit, (South Barrington, Illinois, 2005), video cast.

should be ready to pursue that passion with everything that God created you to be. Now it is time to recap what a life leader is.

Ten Principles of a Life Leader

Throughout the book I have written ten principles that describe what a life leader is. I will take each of those principles and explain them in detail. The most important thing to remember is that life leaders can be anyone from a stay at home mom to the CEO of a company. Everyone has been created with the ability to be a life leader as long as they put the work into becoming totally fit, pursuing their passion, and living out the principles that I will describe in this section.

The original definition of a life leader is someone who leads in every aspect of their own life so effectively that others they come into contact with are motivated to action and inspired to follow. This leads to the first principle to live by as a life leader which is:

1) Work on all five aspects of your own life first.

As you develop these aspects you will soon discover that others will be motivated to not only follow you but also to develop these aspects in their own life. The end result is that as you become a life leader others will see what it has done for you and want to become one too. This leads us to the second principle that a life leader stands by:

2) Contrary to power based leadership principles, life leaders do not use their positions or roles for personal gain. Instead they use their effectiveness as a leader to benefit others they cross paths with in life.

The motivation behind this is that being totally fit allows the life leader to have a high maturity level in all five aspects. Therefore they have more to offer others that have not yet developed these aspects. A life leader is really just a normal person that is working hard to develop the holistic approach to benefit their family, friends, and followers. By normal I mean this person could be anyone you know regardless of their title or position at work, church, or school. You don't have to be successful in your career to become a life leader, but you do have to work towards pursuing your passion and developing the holistic approach. To do this you must take the road less traveled which is principle number three.

When I say that a life leader takes the road less traveled I do not mean that they pursue a chaotic path in life.

3) They should follow a road that requires hard work but reaps more benefits. This path in life is filled with good habits which can only be obtained through a difficult transformation that leaves bad habits behind.

It requires the shedding of our old self and the development of our new self in the form of the holistic approach. The five aspects within the holistic approach do not all have to be mastered completely though to be a life leader which brings up the fourth principle.

4) Life leaders are those who balance all five aspects: spiritual, emotional, mental, physical, and social first and then continually work to improve them together throughout their life.

It is this balanced approach that allows you the best chance of positively influencing your own life and then guiding others to do the same. If you try to master all the areas at first what will end up happening is you will become strong in one or two and neglect the others. You are more effective to be balanced in all five areas of life and then continually working to get better in each then to be great in some and poor in others. If you did become balanced in all of them and wanted to raise your fitness levels further start with understanding principle number five.

5) A life leader is a person who knows how to continually develop their spiritual fitness level throughout their life in order to express the fruits of the spirit for the benefit of others.

This is a principle that must always be followed because it improves your relationship with God who can help you get through the tough challenges required to develop the other aspects. When you have a great relationship with Him, the Holy Spirit allows you to express the

Fruits of the Spirit which can improve your emotional, mental, physical, and social aspects as well. So by continually developing your spiritual maturity you no longer have an average fitness level in any of the other aspects. This spiritual maturity also allows the life leader to guide others through their spiritual journey using the Fruits of the Spirit and knowledge from the Bible. Often a life leader will run into followers that struggle with their own emotional fitness level which is why principle number six should be followed.

6) Life leaders take into account that they have both healthy and unhealthy emotions in their general makeup and then focus on expressing healthy ones.

As human beings that were created by God we inherited strong emotions from Him. A life leader should learn to express the emotions that are similar to those shown by God. The healthy emotions that should be expressed to others are: compassion, love, forgiveness, happiness, sympathy, and gladness. If unhealthy emotions do become a problem in your life then you should seek a support system to get to the root of the problem. Or if you know someone that is struggling with unhealthy emotions then you can be their support system and show them how to get to the root of the problem. A life leader is not afraid to use their knowledge and emotional stability to help others at a lower emotional health level. This leads us to the seventh principle a life leader should follow in order to have the knowledge they need to help others.

7) A life leader is someone that learns how to become mentally fit by continually developing their mind in all areas in order to function as a holistic thinker.

Just make sure that you have already transformed your mind by accepting the Holy Spirit as part of your spiritual development. This will allow you to become more of a holistic thinker like God intended you to be and to not use knowledge for your own personal gain. Instead you will be using the developed mind to pass knowledge on to others without expecting anything in return. This will benefit others who rely on you to help solve problems, make decisions, and look out for their best interest. Life leaders also learn how to improve upon the weak areas of their brain in order to develop the minds of their followers later on. But a strong mind without a strong body does not allow us to be totally fit which brings about the eighth principle.

8) *Life leaders are those who keep themselves physically fit in order to be better prepared to serve those around them.*

Often followers will respect a leader more if they are in better physical health and take care of their body. Being in shape also allows you to have more energy, better posture, and even more confidence. It also allows you to avoid more diseases and handle stress better. Followers will notice these things and be influenced and motivated to become more physically fit in their own lives. So once you are physically fit you should work to teach others to do the same. While you are doing this you should also learn to live by principle number nine.

9) *A life leader is a person who knows how to have a healthy social life that benefits them and their followers.*

God created all of us to be social beings that thrive in relationships with others. To have a healthy social life you must embrace two different groups of people. The first is an inner circle that has similar values to you and can act as a support system both during your development and later as you pursue your passion. The second is made up of individuals who are very diverse in nature and are selected based on who needs your help. You should show them love and compassion and demonstrate what it means to be a socially fit person that can help others in need. When we love others the diversity barrier comes down and the chance for successfully guiding others goes up. A life leader also uses the diversity of a social group to bring together great ideas that can help anyone else who is in need of development. To combine all of these principles you should follow the tenth and final one below.

10) *A life leader is someone who develops all five aspects weekly.*

With busy lifestyles this means using effective time management to develop some of the areas at the same time. To make time to improve all aspects on a weekly basis you must block off time on your schedule to develop the things that matter most in your life. These include development activities in the following areas: God, family, health, work, school, and social activities. Following your new schedule will be tough but the result of obtaining total fitness is the production of synergism. This synergy is what makes the holistic approach to becoming a life leader so effective when it comes time to pursue your passion. Now that we have discussed all these aspects and principles in detail it is time to put what you have learned into practice.

A Call to Action

At this point I am going to assume that you have read the previous chapters and understand the concepts that have to be developed to become a life leader. If it has been awhile, then go back and review the lessons learned at the end of each chapter. You also may or may not know what your passion is in life. If you do, great; if not, I have provided a guide at the end of this chapter for you to begin to determine that. Understanding all of this is important before attempting to put the life leadership principles into practice. The reason for this is that I want life leaders to fill the leadership deficit in the world. The mission statement below was written shortly after the name life leader was associated with my vision. It will be used as the foundation of my Life Leaders consulting business and shows you how important all of this is to me.

> Life Leaders is committed to alleviating the world's leadership deficit by training and coaching the next generation of leaders to be holistically prepared to face all personal and professional challenges. This holistic approach centers on motivating individuals to be spiritually, emotionally, mentally, physically, and socially fit to lead their families, communities, churches, businesses, and schools. Life Leaders promote positive influence by using their innate gifts and calling to serve others with the highest caliber of ethical integrity.

This mission statement sums up my passion to train and coach as many life leaders as possible in order to make up for the deficit left by poor leaders in the world. This calling comes from God and will require me to continually develop all aspects of my life in order to set a good example for others. Writing this book is part of that calling and it is my hope that I have influenced you enough to make a change in your life and pursue your passion.

So please join me in developing the next generation of great leaders that serve others without expecting anything in return. I truly believe that together we can not only change our life but the lives of others. The concepts are simple, as they take us back to God's original plan for our life. The work involved is not as simple, as you take the road less traveled but it will make all the difference as you become who God created you to be in the first place. Thank you for taking this journey with me and I wish you success as you apply life leadership.

Determining Your Passion

If you already know your passion then you can skip this section and go on to the Appendix to view the four workouts. If you have struggled with finding your passion then answer the questions below in the space provided. Remember your passion is something that burns deep inside of you so much that you can't stand it until you do something about it throughout most of your life.

1) What are some of the major things in life that frustrate you so much that you wish you could dedicate your life to addressing?
    An example: Poor leadership frustrates me so I will now dedicate my life to teaching others about the right kinds of leadership. List your own frustrations in life.

2) Which of the items listed in question #1 could you realistically pursue if you started working towards getting the proper training and resources needed to address that frustration?

3) What steps can you take in the next six months to begin to prepare yourself to pursue this passion?

Make sure you will enjoy addressing this frustration for years to come. A passion should be something you would do even if it doesn't make as much as your current job. The reason being is that our passion burns deep inside of us and that fuels greatness which needs to be unleashed and pursued. So have fun and good luck on your journey.

Appendix

Four Exercise Routines

Workout #1: For Men Exercising At Home

Day 1: Chest & Biceps
- Push-ups - 4 sets 15 reps
- Dumbbell Flies - 4 sets 15 reps
- Dumbbell Incline Press - 4 sets 15 reps
- Seated Dumbbell Curls - 4 sets 15 reps
- Preacher Curls - 4 sets 15 reps
- Dumbbell Hammer Curls - 3 sets 20 reps

Day 2: Legs
- Lunges with Dumbbells - 4 sets 15 lunges each leg
- Pump Squats - 4 sets 20 reps & 10 pumps
- Dumbbell Dead Lifts - 4 sets 15 reps
- Single Leg Calf Raise - 4 sets 20 reps

Day 3: Back & Triceps
- Dumbbell Dead Lifts - 4 sets 15 reps
- Bent Over Rows - 4 sets 15 reps
- Dumbbell One Arm Row - 4 sets 15 reps for each arm
- Dumbbell Overhead Extensions - 4 sets 15 reps
- Dumbbell Kickbacks - 4 sets 15 reps for each arm
- Dips Legs - 4 sets 20 reps or till failure

Day 4: Shoulders
- Dumbbell Shoulder Press - 4 sets 15 reps
- Seated Dumbbell Lateral Raises - 4 sets 15 reps

- Dumbbell Front Raises - 4 sets 15 reps
- Upright Row with Curl Bar - 4 sets 15 reps
- Dumbbell Bent Over Rear Delts - 4 sets 15 reps

- All four days warm up with abs and push-ups. Do 4 sets of crunches till failure with one minute break between sets. Then do 3 sets of push-ups till failure with one minute break between sets.
- For the workout use slow controlled movements. Take one minute breaks between sets.
- Better technique better results. Also the weight you choose should be challenging enough that you feel the exercise and are sore the next day.

Workout #2: For Women Exercising At Home

With Ball (3 Day Routine)
- Arm curls (seated on the ball arms at the same time) - 1 set 15 to 20
- Lateral raises (seated on the ball arms raise to the side) - 1 set 15 to 20
- Shoulder press (seated on the ball arms raise above your head) - 1 set 15 to 20
- Kickbacks (seated on the ball lean forward arms behind you) - 1 set 15 to 20
- Chest press (upper back on ball arms in front of you) - 1 set 15 to 20
- Chest flies (upper back on ball arms like hugging a tree) - 1 set 15 to 20

Without Ball (3 Day Routine)
- Upright rows (arms in front raise like an elevator) - 1 set 15 to 20
- Dead lifts (legs bent back straight) - 1 set 15 to 20
- Dead lifts (legs straight back straight feet together) - 1 set 15 to 20
- Lunges (each leg knees behind toes) - 10 to 15

- Pump squats (20 full 10 pumps knees behind toes) - 20 sets of 10
- Jumping jacks - 50 to 100

- All three days warm up with 15 minutes of speed walking or jogging and abs. Bicycle crunches 2 sets 15 to 20 reps. Ball crunches 2 sets 15 to 20 reps. Leg raises with ball between legs 2 sets 10 to 15 reps.
- Note: Every week try to increase the length of time and distance of cardio. Try to progress in 5 minute intervals working up to 45 minutes to an hour. Challenge yourself with different speed intervals. Ex. Your body works like a car does in comparison to gas mileage. Cars burns more fuel around town because all the stop and go. Well your body works the same way by high and low heart rate. Challenge yourself for a minute or two and then back it off for a minute or two. The formula for calculating heart rate range is 220 minus your age times .85 for cardio and times .65 for fat burn. Ex. 36 year old male or female (220 - 36 X .85 = 156.4) (220 – 36 X .68 = 119.6)
- Abs: Don't rush, instead go slow and really contract your abs through the crunches. You should try your best to contract your abs throughout the entire workout. The sets and reps I suggested is just a starting point. Everyone is different if you can do more than 15 or 20 reps go for it.
- In this routine you're going to do each exercise back to back with no break. After the full rotation you will take a 60 to 90 second break, and then start the second rotation. The purpose is to keep your heart rate elevated. If you feel like you can do more than two rotations go for it. But don't push yourself too hard, instead gradually work into it and remember nobody gets overnight results. As for the weights start with 5 pounds in each hand or resistance bands. These really make you use your abs during your workout. All the exercises need to be done with slow controlled technique so don't rush and try to contract the muscles.

Workout #3: For Men Exercising At the Gym

Day 1: Full Body Routine
- Squats - 1-3 sets for 15 reps
- Bench Press - 1-3 sets for 15 reps
- Dumbbell Shoulder Presses - 1-3 sets for 15 reps
- Machine Row - 1-3 sets for 15 reps
- Barbell Curls - 1-3 sets for 15 reps
- Triceps Push Downs - 1-3 sets for 15 reps
- Calf raises (standing) - 1-3 sets for 15 reps
- Crunches-Abs - 1-3 sets for 15 reps

Day 2: Off

Day 3: Full Body Routine
- Squats - 1-3 sets for 15 reps
- Bench Press - 1-3 sets for 15 reps
- Dumbbell Shoulder Presses - 1-3 sets for 15 reps
- Machine Row - 1-3 sets for 15 reps
- Barbell Curls - 1-3 sets for 15 reps
- Triceps Push Downs - 1-3 sets for 15 reps
- Calf raises (standing) - 1-3 sets for 15 reps
- Crunches-Abs - 1-3 sets for 15 reps

Day 4: Off

Day 5: Full Body Routine
- Squats - 1-3 sets for 15 reps
- Bench Press - 1-3 sets for 15 reps
- Dumbbell Shoulder Presses - 1-3 sets for 15 reps
- Machine Row - 1-3 sets for 15 reps
- Barbell Curls - 1-3 sets for 15 reps
- Triceps Push Downs - 1-3 sets for 15 reps
- Calf raises (standing) - 1-3 sets for 15 reps
- Crunches-Abs - 1-3 sets for 15 reps

- This is a beginner's workout for a man that has just joined a gym. This exercise should be used with machines with cables or with free weights. The recommendation is to do this full body routine for the first 6 to 8 weeks in order to get the muscles used to working out again. Low to moderate weight should be used and increased by 2 to 5 lbs each week as you become stronger. If you are not familiar with the machines or free weights in a gym then ask for a free tour by the staff where they will explain what they are and how to use them. Or use an internet search engine to look up the names and how to do them.

Workout #4: For Women Exercising At the Gym

Day 1: Cardio and Toning
- 5 minute walking warm up on treadmill
- 10 minute Jog on treadmill
- 5 minute walking cool down
- Lat pull downs - 1-3 sets for 15 reps
- Bicep curls - 1-3 sets for 15 reps
- Triceps pushdowns with rope - 1-3 sets for 15 reps
- Dumbbell front raises - 1-3 sets for 15 reps

Day 2: Off

Day 3: Cardio and Core Muscles
- 5 minute walking warm up on treadmill
- 10 minute Interval training on treadmill
- 5 minute walking cool down on treadmill
- Crunches on swiss ball - 1-3 sets for 15-25 reps
- Planks (pushup position on forearms) - 1-3 sets hold for 60 sec.
- Leg raises - 1-3 sets for 15 reps

Day 4: Off

Day 5: Cardio and Lower Body Workout
- 5 minute walking warm up on treadmill
- 10 minute Jog on treadmill
- 5 minute walking cool down on treadmill
- Swiss ball squats - 1-3 sets for 15 reps
- Forward lunges - 1-3 sets for 15 reps
- Lying leg curls - 1-3 sets for 15 reps
- Lying Abduction - 1-3 sets for 15 reps
  (Lying on your side on the ground lifting one leg above the other and back down)

Day 6: 30 Minute Walk on Track, Outside, or on Treadmill

Day 7: Off
- This is a beginner's workout for women who have just joined a gym. Take the free tour at the gym to learn more about the various workouts listed or do an internet search on the names. This workout can be done for the first 6 to 8 weeks before switching your routine. The reason you should switch after this time period is to shock the muscles and keep them from hitting a plateau.

Reference List

Bass, B. *Improving organizational effectiveness through transformational leadership.* Newbury Park, CA: Sage Publications, 1994.

Bell, Chip R. *Managers as Mentors- Building Partnerships for Learning, Second Edition.* San Francisco: Barrett-Koehler publishers, Inc., 2001.

Bellsouth. "E-Merger News Letter on Diversity." *Integration News.* Atlanta, December 20, 2006.

Blanchard, Ken & Hodges, Phil. *The Servant Leader.* Nashville, TN: Thomas Nelson, 2003.

Blessitt, Arthur. "How Far Did Jesus and Mary Walk." *The Official Website of Arthur Blessitt.* http://www.blessitt.com/?q=miles_jesus_and_mary_walked (accessed January 18, 2009).

Blocher, Henri. *In the Beginning.* Edited by David Preston. Downers Grove, IL: Intervarsity Press, 1984.

Bryman, A. *Charisma and leadership in organizations.* Newbury Park, CA: Sage Publications, 1992.

Burns, J. M. *Leadership.* New York, NY: Harper & Row, 1978.

Crossway Bibles. *The Holy Bible: English Standard Version.* Wheaton, IL: Good News Publishers, 2001.

Doran, George T. "There's a S.M.A.R.T. Way to Write Management's Goals and Objectives." *Management Review,* November 1981: 35.

Frost, Robert. *Mountain Interval.* New York: Henry Holt and Company, 1920.

Harvard Business School. *What Makes a Good Leader.* June 2007. http://hbswk.hbs.edu/item.jhtml?id=2121&t=leadership&noseek=one (accessed June 20, 2007).

Harvard University. "What Is The Cognitive Rift Between Humans And Other Animals?" *Science Daily.* February 22, 2008.

http://www.sciencedaily.com/releases/2008/02/080217102137.htm (accessed December 30, 2008).

Heidebrecht, Doug. "The Renewal of Perception: Romans 12:2 and Post Modernity." *Direction Journal* 25, no. 2 (Fall 1996): 54-63.

Herrmann International. "Genesis of the HBDI." http://www.hbdi.com/WholeBrainProductsAndServices/thehbdi.cfm (accessed January 3, 2009).

Hermann International. "Overview of the HBDI Profile Package." http://www.hbdi.com/WholeBrainProductsAndServices/thehbdi.cfm (accessed January 3, 2009).

Herrmann, Ned. *The Creative Brain: revised edition.* Lake Lure, NC: Brain Books Publishing, 1990.

Hybels, Bill. "Passion." *The Leadership Summit.* South Barrington: Willow Creek Community Church, 2005.

Lumsdaine, Edward, and Monika Lumsdaine. *Creative Problem Solving: Thinking Skills For A Changing World.* Edited by B.J. Clark and Margery Luhrs. New York: McGraw-Hill, Inc., 1995.

Merenvitch, J. & Reigle, D. "Toward a Multicultural Organization". 24 July 2008. <http://www.visions-inc.org/articles.htm>.

Merriam-Webster. *Webster's New Collegiate Dictionary.* Springfield, MO: G. & C. Merriam Co., 1956.

"Multiculturalism". *VISIONS, Inc.* 23 July 2008. <http://www.visionsinc.org/printfriendly/printpage.php>.

Nouwen, Henri J.M. *The Return of The Prodigal Son.* New York, New York: Doubleday, 1992.

Science Daily. "Cognition." December 25, 2008. http://www.sciencedaily.com/articles/c/cognition.htm (accessed December 27, 2008).

Shaw, William H. *Moral Issues in Business.* Australia: Wadsworth, 2001.

U.S. Department of Health and Human Services. *Physical activity and health: a Report of the Surgeon General.* Atlanta: National Center for Chronic Disease·Prevention and Health Promotion, 1996.

U.S. Dept. of Health and Human Services. "About BMI Calculator: English." *Centers for Disease Control and Prevention.* http://www.cdc.gov/nccdphp/dnpa/healthyweight/assessing/bmi/adult_BMI/english_bmi_calculator/bmi_calculator.htm (accessed January 17, 2009).

U.S. Dept. of Health and Human Services. "Marriage and Divorce." *National Center for Health Statistics.* 2008. http://www.cdc.gov/nchs/fastats/divorce.htm (accessed November 20, 2008).

U.S. Dept. of Health and Human Services. "U.S. Obesity Trends 1985-2007." *Centers for Disease Control and Prevention.* 2007.

http:www.cdc.gov/nccdphp/dnpa/obesity/trend/maps/index.htm (accessed January 17, 2009).

University of Missouri-Columbia. "Selflessness-Core of All Major World Religions-Has Neuropsychological Connection." *Science Daily.* December 25, 2008. http://www.sciencedaily.com/ release/2008/12/081217124156.htm (accessed December 27, 2008).

Zondervan Corporation. *New International Version Archaeological Study Bible: An Illustrated Walk Through Biblical History and Culture.* Grand Rapids, MI: Zondervan, 2005.

About the Author

Dr. Jonathan Mayhorn currently works for AT&T as a Lean Six Sigma Master Black Belt, where he coaches those who lead projects to improve processes in the Construction and Engineering Department. Jonathan also teaches five classes in the Systems Engineering Department at the University of North Carolina at Charlotte (UNCC) that focus on leadership, project management,  and systems engineering. Jonathan is also a faculty associate for the Center of Lean Logistics and Engineered Systems (CLLES) at UNCC, where he teaches Lean Six Sigma certification classes. His educational background includes a bachelor's in mechanical engineering and a master's in engineering management, both from UNCC. He also holds a doctor of strategic leadership degree from Regent University. He is a certified Project Management Professional as well. Jonathan lives in Charlotte, North Carolina, with his wife and their three children.